REVIVALS
~ 101 ~

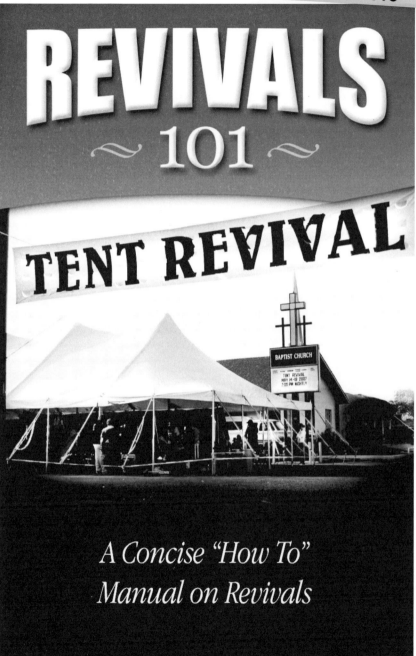

A Concise "How To"
Manual on Revivals

FRANK R. SHIVERS

III

REVIVALS 101:
A CONCISE MANUAL ON THE "HOW TO" OF REVIVAL
published by Victory Hill Publishing Company

© 2008 by Frank Shivers Evangelistic Association
International Standard Book Number: 1-878127-07-1

Cover design by Click-Graphicsonline.com
Editor: Dan Hazlett

Unless otherwise noted, Scripture quotations are from
The Holy Bible *King James Version*

For information
Victory Hill Publishing Company
PO Box 1601
Sumter, South Carolina 29151
www.frankshivers.com

Library of Congress Cataloging –in- Publication Data

Shivers, Frank R., 1949 –
Revivals 101: A Concise Manual on the
"How To" of Revival / Frank Shivers
ISBN # 1-878127-07-1

Library of Congress Control Number:
2007939628

Printed in the United States of America

Dedicated to Junior Hill who has blazed the trail in revivals, seeking to win the lost and bring renewal to the saint for forty years as an evangelist with integrity, humility, compassion and Biblical soundness.

VI

Table of Contents

VIII

Foreword

A very sincere, but obviously discouraged pastor recently said to me, "Old fashioned revival meetings no longer work. I am convinced that in our present culture they are a waste of time." Based upon the rapidly developing trends that are unfolding before us, that bold and frank assessment is by no means an isolated opinion. Many religious leaders and writers have already signed the death certificate for revival meetings. As a matter of fact, some of them have even preached their funeral!

When I first entered full-time evangelism 40 years ago, almost every church in the country still had revival meetings – and often times many of them even had two every year. Today those types of churches are the exception rather than the rule. In this day when revival meetings have virtually disappeared from the religious scene, Frank Shivers' book *Revivals 101* is like a breath of fresh air. In simple, short, and concise words, this seasoned and experienced evangelist has assembled an unusually helpful manual for those who have never attempted a revival meeting as well as those who have. Frankly, it is one of the best presentations I have seen. It is much more than pious rhetoric from someone who has no idea what he is talking about – rather it is the heartfelt sharing of wise and thoughtful principles that have been constantly used and repeatedly proven over and over by this anointed evangelist.

This small volume will be especially helpful for young pastors who are just beginning their ministries and who may not be familiar with some of the tried and proven methods historically used in reaching the lost through revival meetings. Every pastor who is interested in having a revival effort should carefully read this book – and read it before having the meeting! It will not only give wonderful insights into *what to do* but will also wisely warn about some things *not to do*.

If every pastor in this country would read this book and earnestly and prayerfully follow the suggestions set forth, I am thoroughly convinced our churches would immediately see a dramatic and surprising increase in the number of souls won to faith in Jesus Christ. May the dear Lord of Heaven grant that it shall be.

Evangelist Junior Hill
Hartselle, Alabama

IX

Preface

As a vocational evangelist for 34 years, I realize that most pastors are too busy to engage in a lengthy, detailed plan for revival. With this in mind, I have prepared *Revivals 101* to simplify and condense revival preparation.

In this effort, I have sought not to exclude any key element in revival planning but, when practical, to combine them in order to streamline the process. It is my prayer that this endeavor will prompt more pastors to have revival and give them adequate and necessary preparation. Revivals that are properly planned, prayed, powered and preached are revivals that become productive.

In my early years in evangelism, evangelists would lead in seven- to eight-day revivals. The time came when the revival week was shortened to six days, then to five days, and now to four days. Some pastors have written off revival meetings altogether. In this day of increasing carnality, compromise, and complacency within the church and encompassing spiritual darkness outside the church, may God raise up a generation of ministers who will once again blaze the trail of old-fashioned revival as in the times of Whitefield, Sunday, Wesley, Finney, Moody, Torrey, and Truett. Such days of revival are not something of the past. A "Holy Ghost" Pentecostal Revival yet awaits the pastors and churches that are willing to get serious with God and pay the price for it.

Frank Shivers
Columbia, South Carolina

Back to Revival
Frank Shivers

Back to revival the Church must go, lest she die in her content with the
status quo.
Preaching is weak, attendance is low and the winning of souls is mighty
slow.
Compromise in theology and conduct, too, has stagnated the work God
wants to do.

Prayer altars are empty, aisles cold, and baptism pools dry, yet few in the
membership ever ask why.
Not to offend, some preachers claim, sin no longer by them is called by
name.
Old-time preaching on man's need to repent no longer thunders from the
pulpit with heartfelt intent.

The invitation after the sermon in many pulpits has been deleted, failing to
give man the opportunity to make the spiritual decision that is needed.
Lips are sealed refusing to tell of Jesus and Calvary to those going to Hell.

Youth are leaving the church in masses once they begin their college classes.
Teen baptism has sharply declined revealing efforts to reach them are
lagging behind.
Thousands of preachers each year quit, no longer being spiritually fit.
Revival is the need of the hour; it's time to seek Holy Ghost power.

Back to revival the Church must go, despite the wrangling on of leaders
who say it can never do so.
Some state it was good while it did last but now such meetings are a thing
of the past.
Junior, Bailey, Bill and other evangelists wholeheartedly attest, that God
is not finished with revival meetings as these suggest.
Lives changed and souls won, speak loudly of the work revival has done.
Revival is not the "meeting" understand; it simply provides the opportunity
to experience God's redeeming and restoring hand.

Back to revival let the church depart, to experience the power of God deep
in the heart.

Back to a revival of conviction of sin, that leads to repentance and cleansing within.

Back to a revival of anointed preaching and singing that stirs hearts to contend for God with all their being.

Back to days of revival where people in the pew, are confronted with a need to be made brand new.

Back to days of revival where the 'tares' become true 'wheat,' uniting with the saved to render Satan continual defeat.

Back to days of revival praying that in faith prevails; pleading for souls by name to be saved from Hell.

O to the need of revival may the church quickly awake, scheduling a "meeting" before it's sadly too late.

Chapter One
The Place of Revival

Revival days are not normal days in the life of the church. They are supernormal, supernatural.

—*Wesley Duewel (Duewel, 11)*

Study the history of revival. God has always sent revival in the darkest days. Oh for a mighty, sweeping revival today.

—*Adrian Rogers (Bright, 88)*

Ambiguity exists with the name revival. This name has been used in a dual capacity to include both evangelistic and personal renewal meetings from long before I entered evangelism to the present day. Biblically and ideally, it would be best to call both for what they, in substance, are intended. J. Edwin Orr, the greatest historian on revival who ever lived, sought to undo the error in the dualistic use of the name revival but failed. I will not attempt to do what he could not, so in this volume "revival" will refer to both a renewal for God's people and as an evangelistic means to reach the unsaved. This is the concept that many pastors and most in the pew embrace.

Revivals from their beginning have been an effective means to win the unsaved and reclaim the saved. Revivals in the Bible include the revival at the foot of Sinai (Exodus 32:26-32); revival under Asa (2 Chronicles 15:1-15); revival under Hezekiah (2 Chronicles 29: 1-19); revival under Josiah (2 Chronicles 34:1-7); revival under Ezra and Nehemiah (Nehemiah 8 - 9); revival at a river bank (Acts 16:9-15); revival at Pentecost (Acts 2: 37-47); revival at Ephesus (Acts 19:8-29); revival in a jail (Acts 16:25-34) and a revival in a chariot (Acts 8:26 -40). History attests to great and spiritual profitable revivals led by John and Charles Wesley, D.L. Moody, Evan Roberts, Billy Sunday, C.H. Spurgeon, George W. Truett, E.J. Daniels, J. Harold Smith, John R. Rice, John (Praying) Hyde, Billy Graham, George Whitefield and Jonathan Edwards. God has time and again ordained revivals as means of evangelism and revival. More than 2,700 million people in our world stand in need of Jesus Christ. Revival is a "tried and tested" tool that will assist the Church in reaching them.

Despite the view of some pastors that revivals are a thing of the past, preachers who continue to have them testify otherwise. A pastor stated, "I have heard for many years that revivals are 'on their way out!' During these years, our church has continued to reach people for Christ through revivals. We consistently are among the ten leading churches in our state in baptisms. I hope we never 'learn' that revivals are dead." (Rainer, 32)

A revival meeting is still profitable for the church. It is profitable with regard to the souls that are saved. Though many evangelistic tools are available to reach the lost, revival is yet one of the most effective when implemented biblically, compassionately and urgently. George Sweazey wrote, "His pulpit still offers the minister his supreme evangelistic opportunity. No form of communication the Church has ever found can compare with preaching." (Sweazey, 159) The atmosphere of a revival meeting controlled by the Holy Spirit creates the setting for the unsaved to be convicted and converted. Day-by-day preaching in revival is able to strike the hard rock of man's heart over and over with the gospel hammer until it finally breaks and he is saved. This is undeniable. As God's Word is expounded from pulpit and pew in days of revival, the community is saturated with the gospel, and the result is numeral and spiritual growth. Curtis Hutson evidenced 625 saved in a single service and 1,502 saved in an eight-day revival meeting. (Smith, 94) Revivals yet are an effective evangelistic methodology. Slightly less than half of the most evangelistic churches in America regularly schedule revival meetings. (Rainer, 25)

W.B. Sprague in his excellent volume *Lectures on Revivals* presented what I believe is an irrefutable case for revivals. In part he stated, "Suppose then it be admitted that Christians, on the whole, gain no advantage from revivals, on account of the reaction that takes place in their experience, still there is the gain of a great number of genuine conversions, and this is clear gain from the world. Is it not immense gain to the church, immense gain to the Savior, that a multitude of souls should yield up their rebellion, and become the subjects of renewing grace. And if this is an effect of revivals (and who can deny it?) what becomes of the objection that, on the whole, they bring no gain to the cause?" (Sprague, 41-42)

Thom Rainer, president of LifeWay, reported that in 1950 Southern Baptist churches baptized 376,085 people, which is more than 4,000 above the latest total of 371,850. "Simply stated, the Southern Baptist Convention is reaching no more people today than it did in 1950," Rainer said in that report. ("Despite Urging") Revival leads to baptisms.

Youth baptism and commitment is in decline. In the early 1970's youth baptisms in our churches reached an all time high of close to 138,000. Thirty-five years later, despite increased numbers of trained youth workers, youth baptisms have declined to about 81,000. Last year in our convention, more than 20,000 churches did not baptize one teenager. A Barna study in 2006 reveals that 75 to 88 percent of students involved in youth ministry now "will check out of church during their freshman year in college." (Ledbetter) Revival (youth or church wide) is a "tried and proven" tool for the church in re-claiming, converting and conserving its youth.

Revival is profitable with regard to renewal of the saved. It can transform dead churches into living ones complete with a fresh vision of ministry locally and globally. It can convict members guilty of lethargy, compromise, ill-will, apathy, and stagnation and point them to a higher spiritual plane. Revival can make "old members" new and add new members to the church. It can stir the pot so those like Ephraim that are half-baked can be totally yielded to God. It can produce harmony and unity among the brethren. It refreshes and energizers the weary and discouraged saint. In an hour when only 37 percent of Southern Baptist Church members show up for church on Sunday morning, it is indisputable that revival is needed to quicken the "wheat" and regenerate the "tare."

James Stewart wrote, "A church that needs to be revived is a church that is living below the norm of the New Testament pattern. . . . It is a tragic fact that the vast majority of Christians today are living a sub-normal Christian life. . . . The Church will never become normal until she sees revival." (Drummond, Canvass Cathedral, 428)

Revival can ignite spiritual passion for the lost and expand the church's outreach program. In this alone the value of revival is priceless. Southern Baptists statistics indicate that 92 percent of the members go to heaven without making one earnest evangelistic witness. (Sjorgren, Ping, and Pollock, 38) Under passionate preaching, praying and pleading for the lost in revival services, the coldest of hearts can be inflamed to go and tell the gospel story.

Revival benefits the pastor personally. It encourages, excites, enlightens, and energizes the pastor as the Word is proclaimed, decisions are recorded, and fellowship with the evangelist is experienced. As an evangelist, it is a joy to both minister with and minister to the pastor.

C.H. Spurgeon addressed the impact of true revival upon the pastor in his sermon entitled *The Great Revival*. "But now what are the consequences of a revival of religion? It is said that in America the most sleepy preachers have begun to wake up; they have warmed themselves at the general fire, and men who could not preach without notes, and could not preach with them to any purpose at all, have found it in their hearts to speak right out, and speak with all their might to the people. When there comes true revival, the minister all of a sudden finds that the usual forms and conventionalities of the pulpit are not exactly suitable to the times. 'I must have something good for them,' he says. He just burns that old lot of sermons; or he puts them under the bed and gets some new ones, or gets none at all, but just gets his text, and begins to cry, 'Men and brethren, believe on the Lord Jesus Christ, and you shall be saved.' The old deacons say, 'What is the matter with our minister?' The old ladies, who have heard him for many years and slept in the front of the gallery so regularly, begin to rouse and say, 'I wonder what has happened to him; how can it be? Why, he preaches like a man on fire. The tear runs over his eyes; his soul is full of love for souls.' They cannot make it out. How is all this changed? Why, it is the revival. The revival has touched the minister." (Spurgeon, Spurgeon Sermons, 342-343)

> In responding to the criticism that revivals do not last, Billy Sunday said, "Neither does a bath last, but you need to take one now and then."

"There is nothing better than old-fashioned revivals where the half-asleep Christians wake up; where those who have lost their burden for souls get it back; where those who have quit tithing start again; where those who fail to attend church on Sunday night become faithful. An old-fashioned revival where people get excited about the things of God – there is nothing better!" (Hutson, 97)

When Jonathan Edwards inherited his grandfather's church, it was so dead he described it succinctly as "Dry Bones." (Pratney, 86) Sadly, that's a fitting description of many churches. The church needs to be baptized with a fresh dose of Holy Spirit endued enthusiasm and life. Genuine revival always brings renewed joy, excitement, and expectation. "Dislike of enthusiasm," said D.M. Lloyd-Jones, "is to quench the Spirit. Those...familiar with the history of the Church, and in particular the history of revivals, will know this charge of enthusiasm is one always brought against people most active in a period of revival." (Pratney, 26)

Bobby Welch in a sermon at the Southern Baptist Convention said, "I would urge you: If every church in this convention attempted to have two revivals in one year, it would change everything. You say, 'But we don't do any revivals anymore.' I say to you: If you had two of them, it would do you better." Welch continued, "You say, 'Well, if I said revival, nobody would know what we were talking about.' Well, talk about something they know about, but you give them a revival. Spend a few days trying to visit people, spend a few days trying to share the Gospel, spend a few days preaching the Gospel and watch what God will do." (Kentucky Baptist Convention)

Billy Graham in *Biblical Standard for Evangelists* wrote, "The greatest need for God's people today is a true spiritual revival – a fresh outpouring of the Holy Spirit on the Church, a profound experience and turning from sin, and a deepening commitment to God's will in every aspect of life." (Drummond, Evangelist, 150)

Revival is not an outdated method of evangelism and renewal. Like any successful ministry program, it takes prayer, organization, and work weeks prior to its scheduled date to maximize its effectiveness. Thom Rainer in Effective Evangelistic Churches cited three primary factors for revival success as compiled from a study of churches that utilized revivals effectively. Churches that reap a great evangelistic harvest of souls (1) planned extensively, (2) prayed earnestly, and (3) utilized vocational evangelists. (Rainer, 33) Each of these factors is emphasized in the following chapters.

Chapter Two
The Preaching in Revival

How can we expect non-Christians to awake if we ourselves are not awakened? How can "fire" arise if we ourselves do not "burn"? How shall life be begotten if we ourselves are not truly filled with "life"? — *Erich Sauer* (Ravenhill, 138)

Vance Havner identified the kind of revival preacher needed for this hour when he wrote, "We need a Whitefield, a Finney, a Moody who will preach the whole scale of Bible Truth instead of sawing on one note; who will proclaim a solid, substantial message of sin black and Hell hot and judgment certain and eternity long and salvation free by grace through faith in Christ. There is too much back-fence haranguing and hair-splitting, peddling of knickknacks and sandwiches, when men are dying for the meat of the Word." (Havner, 68)

"Of all the lessons which the eighteenth century revival taught the Church, none was more important than the practical demonstration that scriptural preaching, accompanied by the power of the Spirit of God, is the divine means for extending the kingdom of Christ." (Murray) It yet is.

C.H. Dodd stated that "preach" in the New Testament always means to "evangelize" and that *kerygma*, or "preaching," always refers to speaking to the unsaved. Much of our preaching in the church at the present day would not have been recognized by the early Christians as *kerygma*. It is teaching or exhortation (*paraklesis*), or what they called *homilia,* addressed to a congregation already established in the faith." (Sweazey, 159) *Harper's Bible Dictionary* says *kerygma* has to do more with the content of preaching than its act; the "Good News" of redemption through the death, burial and resurrection of Jesus Christ. *Tyndale Bible Dictionary* says *kerygma* is the "Basic evangelistic message proclaimed by the earliest Christians. More fully, it is the proclamation of the death, resurrection, and exaltation of Jesus that leads to an evaluation of his person as both Lord and Christ, confronts one with the necessity of repentance, and promises the forgiveness of sins."

John Stott stated, "Behind the concept and the act of preaching there lies a doctrine of God, a conviction about his being, his action and his purpose. The kind of God we believe in determines the kind of sermons we preach." (Stott, I Believe, 93) This statement of Stott explains some ministers' lack of preaching about the Blood Atonement, Justification by Faith, Repentance, Sanctification, Judgment, Hell, Heaven, Inerrancy of Scripture, Evangelism & Missions and the Second Coming is because their doctrine of God is flawed.

Leonard Ravenhill stated, "I read of the revivals of the past, great sweeping revivals where thousands of men were swept into the Kingdom of God. I read about Charles G. Finney winning his thousands and his hundreds of thousands of souls to Christ. Then I picked up a book and read the messages of Charles G. Finney and the message of Jonathan Edwards on 'Sinners in the Hands of an Angry God,' and I said, 'No wonder men trembled; no wonder they fell in the altars and cried out in repentance and sobbed their way to the throne of grace!'"

Writing on the subject of preaching in local church revivals, L.R. Scarborough stated, "No shams, substitutes, camouflages, spiritual narcotics, or philosophies of men can, in God's sight, be put in the place of the gospel of a crucified Christ. Songs, homilies, testimonies, and exhortations are good and helpful, but they cannot take the place of virile gospel preaching." Further, he stated that the preacher who "minces, dodges, dallies with, evades, or fails to preach the gospel is a traitor and sinner of the worst sort. If he plays with lost souls on the road to Hell, he joins the devil's Judases and deserves the frown of God and the execrations of outraged Christianity." (Scarborough, 117)

> "Young men, be resurrection preachers to dead churches".
> L.R. Scarborough

C.H. Spurgeon said, "The preacher's work is to throw sinners down in utter helplessness so that they may be compelled to look up to Him who alone can help them." (Comfort, 617)

James Clarke declares, "It is a mystery and privilege to have the opportunity to be a channel for the passage of life of God to man, to be the living contact point of the Holy Spirit; the human agents of divine power. The Spirit-filled preacher can touch the conscience, change the motives, and awake the deep, dormant powers of the human heart as no other man." (Duduit, 525)

Robert Murray M'Cheyne advises the preacher, "Get your texts from God – your thoughts, your words, from God...It is not great talents God blesses so much as great likeness to Jesus. A holy minister is an awful weapon in the hand of God. A word spoken by you when your conscience is clear, and your heart full of God's Spirit, is worth ten thousand words spoken in unbelief and sin." (M'Cheyne, Back cover)

Revival Preaching

1. It should be positive. Revival preaching accentuates the positive not the negative. It is not degrading but lifting. Sin must be addressed but ever couched in the love and mercy of a gracious God who stands ready to forgive and redeem. Robert. W. Dale said to G. Campbell Morgan, "I think I have only known one evangelist that I felt had the right to speak of a lost soul. It was D.L. Moody, and it was because he never spoke of the possibility of a man being lost without tears in his voice." Commenting on Dale's statement, Morgan declared, "He (Moody) turned from fiery denunciation of sin into quiet plaintive tearful heart-broken constraint. It is the great secret." (Campbell, 59)

2. It should be personal. Henry Ward Beecher said, "The longer I live, the more confidence I have in those sermons preached where one man is the congregation; where one man is the minister; where there is no question as to who is meant when the preacher says "Thou art the man!" Charles Haddon Spurgeon could preach to audiences of 3,000 or 23,000 and make everyone present feel as if he was speaking to him personally. (Blackwood, 163) Daniel Webster declared, "When a man preaches to me, I want him to make it a personal matter, a personal matter, a personal matter! (Broadus, 165) John Wesley "Seemed to see into men's souls, putting his finger on hidden sins. People felt as if Wesley was speaking to them alone." (Duewel, 89) A person saved in a London crusade said of the preaching of Billy Graham, "I felt as though I was the only person in the arena,

and that every word was meant for me."

3. It should be passionate. The evangelist should preach as to not preach again and as a dying man to a dying people. Leonard Ravenhill declared, "Scholarship on fire is the eighth wonder of the world." (Ravenhill) A revival preacher must be an "eighth wonder" of the world. He must dispense the Holy Scripture with scholarship and compassion. Heartless preaching avails nothing. John Stott stated, "But we should not fear genuine emotion. If we can preach Christ crucified and remain altogether unmoved, we must have a hard heart indeed. More to be feared than emotion is cold professionalism, the dry, detached utterance of a lecture which has neither heart nor soul in it." (Stott, Preacher's Portrait, 51) It is he who speaks with a fire in his bosom and tears in his eye who is able to be used of God to draw men to Christ. E.J. Daniels said that when one of his revival sermons lost fire he threw it in the fire.

4. It should be plain. A veteran minister once gave some sound advice to a young preacher when he told him to keep preaching on the simple but great texts of the Bible, making it clear to people how to be saved. That's advice I have sought to heed throughout my ministry. Revival is not the time to proclaim great theological treatises that seek to impress but to simplify the gospel message in order to bless. Vance Havner humorously said that a theologian was someone who made something simple complicated. The church needs revival preachers who put the message on the bottom rung.

Gyspy Smith declared that preachers are sometimes "more interested upon saying the smart thing than the saving thing." (Breed, 409) Preach the 'saving thing' and do so plainly.

5. It should be penetrating. Revival preaching is Holy Spirit empowered preaching. It should cut to the quick of a man's heart and conscience leading him to see his sinful condition and need of salvation. Preaching that does not reach the conscience is futile and only preaching endued from on high by the Holy Spirit can accomplish this. John Stott stated, "But if human beings are in reality spiritually and morally blind, deaf, dumb, lame and even dead, not to mention the prisoners of Satan, then it is ridiculous in the extreme to suppose that by ourselves and our merely human preaching we can reach or rescue people in such a plight. Only Jesus Christ by his Holy Spirit can open blind eyes and deaf ears, make the lame walk and the dumb

speak, prick the conscience, enlighten the mind, fire the heart, move the will, give life to the dead and rescue slaves from Satanic bondage. And all this he can and does, as the preacher should know from his own experience." (Stott, I Believe, 329)

W.B. Sprague said, "It is only when men are made to feel that the gospel comes home to their individual case, that they are themselves the sinners whom it describes, and that they need the blessings which it offers, that they hear it to any important purpose." (Sprague, 64)

6. It should be persuasive. It is the goal of preaching to persuade men to be reconciled to God. At the beginning of the sermon and interwoven throughout the sermon the invitation to be saved or recommit should be clearly stated.

7. It should be pointed. The day of hour-long sermons are past, especially in revival meetings. Speakers should attempt to prepare the sermon so that it may be proclaimed in thirty minutes or less. I heard Billy Graham preach a six-minute sermon, yet hundreds responded to the invitation. John Bisagno commented that preachers should preach shorter sermons and give longer invitations.

8. It should be pure. The preacher must proclaim the pure and unadulterated Word of God. "What the preacher says, regardless of how logical and dynamic, will not be as effective as the Word of God." (Autry, 120) It is the preaching of the Word that is the "power of God unto salvation." (Romans 1:16) The Bible is a hammer that breaks (Jeremiah 23:29); a sword that cuts (Hebrews 4:12); a fire that burns (Jeremiah 20:9); and a light that illuminates (Psalm 119:105). Given the chance, the Word will break up the hardest soil, cut the most stubborn heart asunder, burn and consume the dross of the most hideous sin, sift from one's life its every contaminate, and illumine the darkest mind of the need of Jesus. Preaching may be expository, topical or textual, but it must always be scriptural. "A sin-sick soul needs a 'thus saith the Lord.'" (Leavell, 106) "To this end we shall continue to preach Christ crucified, because what is folly to the intellectualist and a stumbling-block to the moralist, remains the wisdom and the power of God" (1 Corinthians 1:23-24). (Stott, "Fundamentalism," 37)

9. It should be practiced. One pitcher may earn over $2 million a year for delivering a baseball across home plate while another pitcher

at the same time is delivering the same priced baseball to the same plate for $50,000 a year. The difference is not the baseball but its delivery. (Bisagno, 8) Sadly, too many pastors and evangelists fail to deliver their message effectively. "Their material is excellent; the delivery is poor." (Bisagno, 8) The great pitchers practice continuously throwing a baseball. Practice preaching and delivering the revival sermon. I have rehearsed my sermons before the ocean, stars, mirrors and cow pastures, seeking to burn them in my heart and improve delivery in the church. I have found it profitable to rehearse them time and again upon my knees before God. I am not the preacher I used to be, and by God's grace and my practice, I'm not the preacher I am going to be. The evangelist must continuously work at improving the delivery of the sermon. "All doctrine without polish, illustration, and warm-hearted exhortation would be like a skeleton; all exhortation and illustration without doctrine would be like a jellyfish." (Leavell, 106)

10. It should be prayerful. C.H. Spurgeon recommended preachers pray the same petition as the prophet Elijah on Mt. Carmel. He stated, "Go you to the mercy-seat with this as one of your arguments, 'Lord, I have done according to thy word. Now let it be seen that it is even so. I have preached thy word, and thou hast said, 'It shall not return unto me void.' I have prayed for these people, and thou hast said, 'The effectual fervent prayer of a righteous man availeth much;' let it be seen that this is according to thy word.'" Revival preaching is developed in prayer, decided through prayer, and delivered by prayer but is doomed without prayer.

11. It should be presuming. Revival preaching is expectant, anticipatory of God showing up to perform His mighty works. "Pessimism paralyzes power in evangelistic preaching; but this great optimism of the indwelling of Christ is a perpetual power." (Morgan, 61) One of Spurgeon's "preacher boy" students approached him saying, "Dr. Spurgeon, I am awfully discouraged. Others get up and preach and testify, and souls are saved. But when I speak, testify or preach, nothing ever happens. Why is it that no one is ever saved when I speak?" The great preacher asked the struggling student, "Son, do you expect someone to be saved every time you preach?" The boy answered, "No, not always, Brother Spurgeon, but I do wish someone would be saved now and then." Spurgeon responded, "Young man, that is just the reason you get no results; you never expect anything to happen. Have faith!"

W. B. Riley said, "I believe that the spirit of expectation is a psychological influence that reaches the minds and souls of men. I think that a great auditorium is moved when the lone man, the minister, entertains and expresses that spirit of expectation; I know that psychologically it is true that if he does not express it, their expectation is decreased to that extent, and if he does, it is accentuated. And what is expectation of results except another phrase for faith in God?" (Riley, 19)

12. It should be pride-less. Pride can lead the evangelist to "manufacture" decisions by manipulation and perversion of the condition for salvation. Pressure to "produce" placed upon the evangelist by pastors, religious leaders, and church members must not in any way jeopardize his preaching and ministry. G. Campbell Morgan stated, "The true evangelist will be very careful to avoid the possibility of a passion for numbered results spoiling his message. I sometimes fear lest the desire to have large statistical returns may tend to make a man make the way of salvation unduly easy. We have been preaching 'Believe,' and we have not sufficiently said 'Repent,' 'repent,' 'repent,' and we have still to preach this truth, that unless a man will turn to God from idols, then his faith though he boast of it, is dead and worthless." (Morgan, 82-83)

C.H. Spurgeon in his sermon *Spiritual Revival: The Want of the Church* described the kind of revival preacher needed in this hour. "There is preaching, and what is it? 'O Lord, help thy servant to preach, and teach him by thy Spirit what to say.' Then out comes the manuscript, and they read it. A pure insult to Almighty God! We have preaching, but it is of this order. It is not preaching at all. It is speaking very beautifully and very finely, possibly eloquently, in some sense of the word but where is the right down preaching, such as Whitefield's? Have you ever read one of his sermons? You will not think him eloquent; you cannot think him so. His expressions were rough, frequently very coarse and unconnected. There was very much declamation about him; it was a great part, indeed, of his speech. But where lay his eloquence? Not in the words you read, but in the tone in which he delivered them, in the earnestness with which he felt them, in the tears which ran down his cheeks, and in the pouring out of his soul. The reason why he was eloquent was just what the word means. He was eloquent because he spoke right out from his heart, from the innermost depths of the man. You could see when he spoke that he meant what he said. He did not speak as a trade, or as a mere machine, but he preached what he felt to be the truth and what he could not help preaching. When you heard him preach, you could not help feeling that he was a man who would die if he could not preach, and with all his might call to men and say, 'Come! come! come to Jesus Christ, and believe on him!' Now, that is just the lack of these times. Where, where is earnestness now? It is neither in pulpit nor yet in pew..." (Smith, 54)

Jonathan Edwards testified, "I preach with two thoughts in mind: Every person ought to give their life to Christ; and whether or not anyone else gives Christ his life, I will give Him mine." (Knight, 250)

Revival preaching should include proclamation concerning sin, repentance, the Cross, salvation, and personal surrender. Messages on Hell, Heaven, Judgment, the New Birth, Baptism, Personal Revival, and the Second Coming are always relevant. Additionally a message geared to students is extremely effective.

The poet wrote:

A city full of churches
Great preachers, lettered men
Grand choirs, organs' music
If these all fail, what then?
Good workers, eager, earnest
Who labor hour by hour?
But where, oh where, we ask
Is God's almighty power?
Refinement, education
They have the very best
Their plans and schemes are perfect
They give themselves not rest.
They give the best talents
They try their uttermost
But what they need so clearly
Is God the Holy Ghost.
(Drummond, Canvas Cathedral, 423)

A Revival Questionnaire for the Pastor
It is helpful to the evangelist in his preparation to minister to be acquainted with the church he is to serve. Answers to the following questions by the pastor sent to the evangelist several weeks prior to the revival will be of immense value. What is the purpose of the revival and its goals? When did the church last have a revival meeting? Was it attended greatly, fairly or poorly? Has the church ever utilized a vocational evangelist? Where is the church located (rural, suburban, city)? What is the average attendance in Sunday School? What is your vision for the future of the church? Do you have an active visitation/soulwinning program? What steps is the church taking to prepare for the revival?

Profiles of Revival Preachers
A quick look at some of history's greatest revival preachers reveal why God chose to use them mightily. Visit with them, warm your heart by the fire of their passion, and be instructed by their example.

Jonathan Edwards' Revival Preaching
        Gilbert Tennant, a contemporary of Jonathan Edwards, said of Edwards' revival preaching: "He seemed to have no regard to please the eyes of his hearers with agreeable gestures, nor their ears with delivery, nor their fancy with language; but to aim directly at their heart and consciences, to lay open their ruinous delusions, show them their numerous secret, hypercritical shifts in religion and drive them out of every deceitful refuge wherein they had made themselves easy with the form of godliness without the power…His preaching was frequently both terrible and searching." (Pratney, 189) J. Wilbur Chapman said that Edwards was a "mighty logician and his great theme was The Sovereignty of God's Grace in the Salvation of Sinners." (Chapman, Chapter 19) Ralph G. Turnbull said of Edwards, "He used language in preaching which was theological in its judgment and vitriolic in its effect." (Evans, 24) Edwards said in response to his basic appeal of fear in preaching, "Some talk of it as an unreasonable thing to fright persons to heaven, but I think it is a reasonable thing to endeavor to fright persons away from hell. They

stand upon its brink, and are just ready to fall into it, and are senseless of this danger. Is it not a reasonable thing to fright a person out of a house on fire?" (Evans, 25)

W. Glyn Evans, writing on Edwards' style in preaching, stated, "He used no gestures, no shouting, no dramatics. There was no warmth or fervor in his delivery itself. He had no eye contact with his audience, which led one of his parishioners to complain that he looked at the bell rope on the rear wall of the sanctuary 'until he looked it off.' He was especially effective in using the dramatic pause and in distinct pronunciation." (Evans, 26) Edwards began his ministry reading his sermons from a prepared manuscript, but after meeting Whitefield he preached from notes.

John Wesley's Revival Preaching

"It was a precept of Wesley to his evangelists in unfolding their message, to speak first in general of the love of God to man; then with all possible energy so as to search the conscience to its depths, to preach the law of holiness; and then, and not till then, to uplift the glories of the gospel of pardon and of life. Intentionally or not, his directions follow the lines of the epistle to the Romans." (Pratney, 29)

Wesley, in commenting on God's hand upon his preaching, said, "It is indeed the gift of God, and cannot be attained by all the efforts of nature and art united." He continued in stating that at times, "God Himself made the application, and truly God preached to their hearts." (Duewel, 88) Wesley described himself as one who "spoke plain words to plain folks." (Tyson, 201)

Commenting on Wesley's preaching, one person wrote: "What was the secret of Wesley's power as a preacher? He had little imagination, and no descriptive power. He told no anecdotes, as a rule, and certainly fired off no jests. What fitness had he to talk to peasants, to miners, to the rabble of the city, to the slow-thinking farmer drawn from the plough-tail? Yet he stood up, a little, trim, symmetrical figure; his smooth black hair exactly parted; his complexion clear and pure as that of a girl; his hazel eyes flashing like points of steel. And beneath his words the crowd was melted and subdued until it resembled a routed army shaken with fear and broken with emotion; men and women not seldom falling to the ground in a passion of distress. . . . There was something in his discourse—a note in his voice, a flash in his eye—that thrilled the crowd with awe, awe that not seldom deepened into dread. The mood of the speaker was one of perfect calmness. But it was the calm of power, of certainty, of an authority which ran back into the spiritual world." (Drummond, Canvas Cathedral, 414)

Wesley in *The Sermon Register 3*, a personal journal, wrote dates, locations and sermon texts for one third of his itinerant ministry. He preached from the same texts time and again, some more than others indicating which his favorites were. These favorite texts included Matthew 16:26; Mark 1:15; Mark 12:34; Luke 15:7; Luke 16:26; Romans 8:33; 2 Corinthians 5:18. A text that stood out as being preached more often than any other was Revelation 22:17. These were the texts Wesley used to show man his sin and the need to escape the wrath of God through personal repentance and faith in the Lord Jesus Christ. Wesley would incorporate illustrations and stories in his sermons to make them understandable to the common man, staying away from quotations from his favorite Latin authors and classical poets when in engaged in "open air preaching." He spoke clearly and plainly from the heart in pointed sentences urging his hearers to repent. Wesley preached some 45,000 sermons, 80 percent of which were preached in the "open air." Like his contemporary George Whitefield, these sermons were preached without notes. (McGonigle)

Charles Finney's Revival Preaching

Finney's blue eyes were "remarkably piercing, an asset he used unfailingly in persuading hesitant sinners to come to the Savior. A quick, ready smile would often light up his usually sober expression as he imparted spiritual truths." (Evans, 44) A reporter covering one of Finney's revivals stated, "His style of address is singular direct. There is a total absence of display, and a complete forgetfulness, on most occasions at least, of the graces of elocution. There is the most rigid exactness of statement, the severest simplicity, the closest reasoning, and the discourse proceeds step by step, the judgment of the hearer forced along with it, until the end." (Evans, 45) Finney speaking of his own style in preaching commented, "Any time men are in earnest, as a minister should be, their language is, in point, direct and simple. Their sentences are short, cogent, powerful."

Finney stated of preaching under the Holy Spirit's anointing: "If I did not preach from inspiration I didn't know how I did preach. It was a common experience with me… that the subject would open up to my mind in a manner that was surprising to myself. It seemed that I could see with intuitive clearness just what I ought to say, and whole platoons of thoughts, words and illustrations came to me as fast as I could deliver them." (Bright, 87) Finney declared, "Often I went into the pulpit without knowing upon what text I should speak, or a word that I should say."

Finney made great effort to preach utilizing only simple illustrations. He reasoned to people directly, as a lawyer to a jury pleading for a verdict on the spot. (Duewel, 96)

George Whitfield's Revival Preaching

In contrast to Jonathan Edwards' preaching on the terror of God and the judgment, Whitefield preached the "consolations of God, the privileges of His children, and the outpouring of the Spirit on believers." (Duewel, 61)

Whitefield preached "a healing, tender, positive gospel." (Duewel, 61) Daniel Pals said of Whitefield, "The very thing that accounts for his success [was] a deeply populist frame of mind. Almost every one of Whitefield's sermons is marked by a fundamentally democratic determination to simplify the essentials of religion in a way that gives them the widest possible mass appeals." (Essential Whitefield) Whitefield's preaching style included speaking extemporaneously while often running around on the platform; dramatic facial and hand gestures; bluntness and theatrical re-enactments of Bible stories. Paige Patterson attributes Whitfield's awesome success to a "confidence in the word of God," a "zeal for souls" and a unique "animated, dynamic preaching style." (B. Hawkins)

J.C. Ryle described what an average week in the life of Whitefield was like in the winter when "open air meetings" were not possible. "Every Sunday morning, he administered the Lord's Supper to several hundred communicants at half-past six. After this, he read prayers and preached both morning and afternoon. Then he preached again in the evening at half-past five and concluded by addressing a large society of widows, married people, young men and spinsters, all sitting separately in the area of the Tabernacle, with exhortations suitable to their respective stations. On Monday, Tuesday, Wednesday, and Thursday mornings, he preached regularly at six. On Monday, Tuesday, Wednesday, Thursday, and Saturday evenings, he delivered lectures. This, it will be observed, made thirteen sermons a week! And all this time he was carrying on a large correspondence with people in almost every part of the world." (Ryle) It is estimated that Whitefield preached in excess of 18,000 times before his death in 1770.

"Often as I have read his life", wrote C. H. Spurgeon, "I am conscious of distinct quickening whenever I turn to it. He lived. Other men seemed to be only half-alive, but Whitefield was all life, fire, wing, force. My own model, if I may have such a thing in due subordination to my Lord, is George Whitefield; but with unequal footsteps must I follow in his glorious track." (Essential Whitefield)

D.L. Moody's Revival Preaching

"Mr. Moody was especially adapted to his work, first because he was pre-eminently practical in this practical age. He was most direct in his speech; every one knew exactly what he meant; there was no mistake in his utterance. His energy was literally boundless; day and night and night and day he toiled, never seeming to be weary. His earnestness and enthusiasm were contagious and wherever he found an audience dull and lifeless he had only to speak to them a few minutes until they were ready to do anything that he might command. He preached to larger crowds than any man in his generation, and yet it was ever his object and aim to reach the individual rather than the people in a mass." (Chapman, Chapter 19)

Moody made an effort not to "preach" and stated, "If I can only get people to think I am talking with them, and not preaching, it is so much easier to get their attention." He sought to reach man's heart, not his head in preaching. His sentences contained about 17 words and he spoke at a rate of 230 words per minute. In preaching, Moody often held the Bible in one hand and made unplanned gestures with the other. Unlike Billy Sunday, he did not use bodily extremes in his delivery. Moody had the rich voice like a Whitefield needing no amplification in speaking to crowds of thousands. When hearing him preach, one was impressed that he was a man on fire who kept it under control. He had his critics, and one said, "Oh, the way that man does mangle the English tongue! The daily slaughter of syntax at the Tabernacle is dreadful. His enunciations may be pious, but his pronunciations are decidedly off color. It is enough to make Noah Webster turn over in his grave and weep to think that he lived in vain." (Evans, 65-67)

"His messages had no uncertain sound concerning the Gospel. He believed that men were lost without Christ. He told the story of the mother who came into the Eye Infirmary in Chicago and said: "Doctor, there is something wrong with my baby's eyes." He described how the doctor took the child in his arms and carried it to the window, looked at the eyes only a moment, and then, shaking his head, gave the child back again to its mother. "Well, Doctor, what is it?" she said. "Poor woman" he replied, "your baby is going blind; in three months' time he will be stone blind, and no power on earth can ever make him see." Mr. Moody told how the mother held the baby close against her heart and then fell on the floor with a shriek, crying out, "My God! My baby blind! My baby blind! "I can see his face now as he said, the tears rolling down his cheeks: "Would to God, we might all be as much moved as that when we know that our friends are spiritually blind as well as lost!" Because he believed this, he preached as he did, and it was this spirit that literally drove him to Kansas City to preach his last sermon, and then turn his face home to die. He believed in instantaneous conversion; he had no patience at all with the man who thought he must grow better to be saved." (Chapman, Chapter 19)

Billy Sunday's Revival Preaching
Sunday was a "fire-and-brimstone" revival preacher. Subject

matter for his sermons would often be against booze. He preached, "I'm the sworn eternal, uncompromising enemy of the liquor traffic. I've drawn the sword in the defense of God, home, wife, children and native land and I will never sheath it until the undertaker pumps me full of embalming fluid, and if my wife is still alive I think I shall call her to my bedside, and say, 'Nell, when I'm dead, you send for the butcher and skin me and have my hide tanned and made into drum heads and hire men go up and down the line and beat those drums and say, 'My husband Billy Sunday still lives and gives the whiskey gang a run for its money.'"

On Sunday's delivery, Elijah P. Brown stated, "There is but one word at your command that will even remotely indicate his manner... *action!* At one moment he is at one end of his long platform, and before you become used to seeing him there he is at the other, and then quicker than thought he bounds back to the center, giving the desk a solar plexus blow that would knock out a giant. Ever and anon he makes long rapid strides to give it more whacks, until at last a big piece splits off and bounds to the sawdust floor below." His voice was hoarse and often strained to the point of complete collapse. Sunday would begin his sermons crouching like a tiger springing out to preach once the final word of introduction was made."

In his sermon *The Need of Revivals,* Billy Sunday said, "Religion needs a baptism of horse sense. That is just pure horse sense. I believe there is no doctrine more dangerous to the Church today than to convey the impression that a revival is something peculiar in itself and cannot be judged by the same rules of causes and effect as other things. If you preach that to the farmers - if you go to a farmer and say "God is a sovereign," that is true; if you say "God will give you crops only when it pleases him and it is no use for you to plow your ground and plant your crops in the spring," that is all wrong, and if you preach that doctrine and expect the farmers - to believe it, this country will starve to death in two years. The churches have been preaching some false doctrines and religion has died out."

Billy Graham's Revival Preaching
Graham's sermon to some Scottish preachers reveal his style. "Preach with clarity and simplicity. The fact that you shoot over the heads of your congregation doesn't prove you have superior

ammunition. It proves you can't shoot. Preach with your natural voices…You don't talk in a chant. Then why preach that way? This kind of style shows lack of conviction in the pulpit. Make sure you have a gospel to preach. People don't want good advice. They want the good news of Jesus Christ." (Evans, 115)

Graham's sermon structure is simple. It includes six things: an attempt to create guilt, a reminder that guilt is natural and that all are sinners, a statement that there is a solution to the problem of guilt, explanation of the plan of salvation; note on how salvation is obtained, and to close an urgent appeal for man to take the offer God has made. (Evans, 118) His gestures are plentiful and in his earlier years he paced the platform nearly a mile in the course of a sermon. W. E. Sangster said of Graham's preaching, "Homiletically, Billy's sermons leave almost everything to be desired. They are often without discernible structure. Sometimes there is little or no logical progression. Illustrations are few and far between and generally not of the best. Yet in the wake of this 'poor' preaching, I have seen things I never expected to see, things which I doubt any man has seen since the day of Pentecost." Stanley High said, "The single, most convincing explanation of the power of Billy Graham's preaching is that he speaks 'as one having authority.'" (Evans, 114–116)

Things To Avoid in a Revival Service

1. Lengthy or unrelated announcements.
2. Dead spots.
3. Too much programmed.
4. Disturbing distractions.
5. Starting late.
6. Unchecked technical devices.
7. Starting flat.
8. Preaching a second sermon.
9. Negativism.
10. Un-previewed music, skits, drama or testimonials.
11. Altar call lines.
12. Invitation un-preparedness.
13. Unequally yoked participants.
14. Cramping the evangelist on time.
15. Dismissal delay at invitation conclusion.

Chapter Three
The Pleading in Revival

Several things distinguish evangelistic preaching, but one of the most important is that it includes an appeal for decision – an appeal for men and women to decide for Christ.
—Billy Graham (Douglas, Work of an Evangelist, 171)

It is not enough to expound a thoroughly orthodox doctrine of reconciliation if we never beg people to come to Christ.
—John Stott (Stott, Cross, 201)

Revival preaching includes an invitation for personal response at its conclusion. The central purpose in revival preaching is to reach the unsaved and reclaim/refresh the saint. G. Campbell Morgan said in regard to evangelistic preaching, "The business of the evangelist is to get a verdict for Jesus Christ there and then." (Morgan, 82) Jerry Vines stated, "At the end of every sermon I invite people to receive Jesus Christ as their Lord and Savior. I do so on very good Bible precedent. The last page of the Bible has this marvelous invitation. "And the Spirit and the bride say, Come. And let him that heareth say, Come. And let him that is athirst come. And whosoever will, let him take the water of life freely." (Revelation 22:17) (Allen & Gregory, 410)

I have gleaned from my experience as an evangelist and from the writings of learned men on this subject some helps in extending the invitation effectively. I addressed these and numerous others in detail in *The Evangelistic Invitation 101.*

1. It should be extended uniformly.
The invitation must tie in with the sermon without any break or delay. The invitation must flow without interruption straight from the sermon. Avoid "dead spots" between the sermon and the invitation. This is addressed fully in Chapter Four.
2. It should be extended clearly.
The revival preacher must not leave any doubt in the mind of the youngest or oldest in issuing the invitation exactly what decision he is asking them to consider and to make. He must be cautious not to

confuse minds by bunching a lot of different types of decisions together. If the revival preacher's purpose is to invite people to make several different kinds of commitment then he should do so in "piece-meal" fashion, one at a time.

In extending the invitation, the revival preacher must make clear the sinner may come just as they are with sin and all. Often I quote the first stanza of "Just As I Am" and say, "Jesus wants you to come with your baggage, sin and all. He is not intimated by any sin you have committed. He died for it." Emphasize that Jesus waits with open arms for the worst sinner and that no sin is beyond His grace to forgive and no sinner is beyond His power to save.

3.   It should be extended passionately.

The revival preacher must plead with a bleeding heart for the lost to be saved. A burdened heart cannot be faked. C. H. Spurgeon exhorted his preacher boys, "Impressed with a sense of their danger, give the ungodly no rest in their sins; knock again and again at the door of their hearts, and knock as for life and death. Your solicitude, your earnestness, your anxiety, your travailing in birth for them God will bless to their arousing." (Spurgeon, Letters, 345)

4.   It should be extended gently.

Herbert Farmer stated, "The preacher must respect the sacred right of rejection which belongs to all people." God patiently stands at the threshold of man's heart and says, "Behold I stand at the door and knock…"   Farmer warned, "No preacher must go beyond God." (Walker, 63) It is essential that even when a sinner rejects Christ the minister manifests His love.

5.   It should be extended prayerfully.

The revival preacher must pray before extending the invitation, pray while extending it, and pray following it. Prayer ought to permeate the invitation from beginning to end.

Billy Graham stated, "Every time I give an invitation I am in an attitude of prayer inwardly, because I know I'm totally dependent on God." He continued, "This is the part of the evangelistic service that often exhausts me physically. . .there is an inward groaning and agonizing in prayer that I cannot possibly put into words." (Douglas, Work of the Evangelist, 173)

6. It should be extended urgently.

The sinner must be brought to realize that "tomorrow" may be too late to be saved. It is the revival preacher's task under the anointing of the Holy Spirit to show man the deadly danger of delay and thus his need to be saved immediately.

"The little word 'now' is often on the evangelical preacher's lips: 'Now is the accepted time. Now is the day of salvation. Accept Christ now lest you go to Hell.' The word asks, 'Why live another day without the joy, the inner peace, the fulfillment which Christ can bring?' So there is calling for an answer, now." (Walker, 61) The revival preacher must call sinners to repentance and faith in Christ with soul urgency each time the invitation is extended! It may be their last chance to come. Spurgeon stated, "When anyone dies, I ask myself, 'Was I faithful? Did I speak all the truth? And did I speak it from my very soul every time I preached?'" (Comfort, 504) Every evangelist/revival preacher should ask not only these questions but also one more that I would add: "Did I do my very best in drawing the net when he sat before me in the assembly for the last time?"

7. It should be extended thoroughly.

The revival preacher in issuing the invitation must not quit too soon. When is too soon? Ministers die a thousand deaths in the invitation due to the fear of extending it too long or closing it prematurely. He has to stay in tune to the leadership of the Holy Spirit from its start to finish. It is the Holy Spirit alone who can inform the minister when "enough is enough."

8. It should be extended fearlessly.

James Stewart declared, "It is not your personality that has to be impressed redeemingly upon other souls—thank heaven for that; it is not you who dazzle men with your grasp of the truth or your powers as a defender of the faith; it is not you who are going to convert souls and unlock the shining gate to which Jesus has the key. Bring everything you have and are to your ministry—your best craftsmanship, your most concentrated study, your truest technique, your uttermost of self-consecration, your toil and sweat of brain and heart — bring it without reserve. But when you have brought it, something else remains: Stand back and see the salvation of God." (Stewart, 188-189)

9. It should be extended confidently.

One of the surest ways to invite failure in the invitation is for the revival preacher following his appeal to pick up a hymnal and bury his face in it as he stands to receive people. Expect them to come! He is to keep his eyes pealed for sinners edging out of their seats to respond and encourage them as they do. The revival preacher in faith anticipates and expects that sinners will respond. "According to your faith be it unto you." (Matthew 9:29)

10. It should be extended soberly.

This is not to say there is no place for emotion in preaching or the invitation. The emotion, however, should be generated by the Holy Spirit so that it may lead to godly repentance and not a worldly one that does not save. The revival preacher must be careful in his appeal to sinners not to commit what E.M. Griffin of Wheaton College calls "emotional rape." (Turnball, 235)

11. It should be extended earnestly.

The invitation must not be simply a closing addendum but treated with solemnity.

12. It should be extended interwovenly.

The most effective invitation is one that is not simply extended at the end of a sermon but one that is intertwined throughout the sermon. In the introduction or opening prayer, the revival preacher should share what decision he will be asking people to make in response to the sermon. In the body of the message he should occasionally repeat the decision he will be calling on his hearers to make and then, at its conclusion, present the call clearly again.

13. It should be extended open-eddedly.

Following the revival preacher's formal invitation, he should make clear that after the service the invitation still stands. Counselors should be available at the altar when the service has concluded to council private inquirers. It must be made clear both where these counselors will be standing and for how long.

14. It should be extended specifically.

The revival preacher must not be vague but direct regarding what decision he is asking people to make. He must be prepared upon entering the invitation to specifically articulate the response desired of his hearers.

15. It should be extended persuasively.

The Apostle Paul said, "Knowing the terror of the Lord, we persuade men." (2 Corinthians 5:11) This word "persuade" means to "induce one by words to believe." It is in the invitation that the revival preacher's words must be wisely chosen, especially as he seeks to convince sinners of their need to be saved. Knowing what is man's lot presently and eternally without Christ motivates the preacher to persuade them earnestly and passionately to be saved. He must persuade the sinner to choose life over death, heaven over hell, happiness over heartache, good over bad, purity over immorality, Jesus Christ over the world, the flesh and the devil. "A man can be moved to action if his mind can be convinced that the action is reasonable, and if his heart can be convinced that the action is necessary. A revival preacher must therefore bring the hearer to the point where he says, "I can be saved (mind). I must be saved (emotions). I will be saved (will)." (Streett, 159)

No revival preacher should forget that it is the Holy Spirit who uses him to "persuade" the lost that trusting Jesus Christ as Lord and Savior is both reasonable and imperative!

16. It should be extended helpfully.

The revival preacher should make response as easy as possible for the hearer of his sermon. He can do this in three ways: first, by declaring exactly what he wants them to do, how, and when; second, by asking those in the pews to step back to make room for people to walk pass; and, third, by making known what will happen when a person arrives at the altar. Settling a lot of uneasiness about the mechanics of coming to the altar in a sinner's mind is imperative. The fear of the unknown in responding to an invitation is a barrier to one's salvation the minister can easily remove.

17. It should be extended unassumingly.

Thirty-four years of evangelistic ministry has taught me to never assume anything regarding the invitation. Revival preachers don't assume the musicians know when to play. Don't assume the host pastor knows not to interrupt your appeal until you are finished. Don't assume the song leader, choir, or soloist will select an evangelistic song to sing. The revival preacher should get to the church, tent, or assembly area early and personally make sure everything is ready to go without a hitch.

18. It should be extended readily.

"Waiting lines" during invitations may hinder others from responding and must be avoided by having sufficient counselors in place. These trained and equipped saints should ever be alert to the signal of the revival preacher or pastor to move forward to provide assistance.

19. It should be extended personally.

O.S. Hawkins in *Drawing the Net* stated, "An analysis of the first recorded appeal of Simon Peter (Acts 2), and the first recorded appeal of the apostle Paul (Acts 13) reveals an interesting insight. When it was time to <u>draw the net</u> they moved from first- and third-person pronouns to second-person pronouns at the critical point of the appeal. Consider Simon Peter standing on the temple mount in Jerusalem. Hear him appeal, This man was handed over to **you** by God's set purpose and foreknowledge; and **you**, with the help of wicked men, put him to death by nailing him to the cross (Acts 2:23, author's italics). Hear the great apostle Paul speaking in the synagogue at Antioch: Therefore, my brothers, I want **you** to know that through Jesus Christ the forgiveness of sins is proclaimed to **you**" (Acts 13:38, author's italics). Your proclamation of the good news must have a personal appeal. Like Peter and Paul, you should not merely aim at the head but also at the heart. This type of appeal convicts the hearts of hearers. After Peter finished his appeal the Bible reports, "When the people heard this, they were cut to the heart." (Acts 2:37) (O.S. Hawkins, 30)

That is the reason we have so many "mushroom" converts, because their stony ground is not plowed up; they have not got a conviction of the Law, they are stony-ground hearers.
— George Whitefield (Comfort, 269)

Chapter Four
The Praise in Revival

We need songs that stir people to win souls, songs that call people to consecration, songs that plead with sinners to turn from their sin and warn sinners of the dangers of delay and of judgment.
—*John R. Rice* (Rice, 131)

Ira Sankey was an accomplished pianist, music composer, and song leader who stood by D.L Moody's side for over 25 years in evangelistic meetings. D.L. Moody said that Ira Sankey had sung far more people into the Kingdom than he ever preached into it. That statement by one of history's greatest harvest evangelists underscores the important position of a revival/crusade music leader. Dr. T. B. Lackey told John Bisagno, "A good song service is half the battle any day." (Bisagno, 26) I wholeheartedly agree. Much too often the evangelist has to gather his own sticks and build his own fire in a revival due to the cold and lifeless singing that precedes him.

"Music is of the utmost importance. It can make or break the services. Church music is not an end in itself – it is a device for producing certain spiritual results; it is an instrument for opening hearts to religious influences; it is a vehicle for taking religious truths into minds; it is a form of religious expression." (Sweazey, 178-179) Sweazey continued, "Evangelism is sadly handicapped by the music in many of our churches – something to be endured, not enjoyed." (Sweazey, 179) W. B. Riley wrote, "More than once I have been in services where the opening songs and prayer had little or no relation to the soul-winning intent. And occasionally I have been in services where a good soul-winning sermon was preached, but a wretched choice of a hymn that had no decision in it and sometimes was even destitute of salvation suggestion, was sung at the close. Such action is a decision killer." (Riley)

Charlie Alexander was the song leader for R. A. Torrey and J. Wilbur Chapman. In this position, he met with great success because he determined that his songs would harmonize with the sermon these men preached, "and his closing hymns were always chosen with reference to fastening the nail that had been driven by the minister, in a sure place." (Riley) "Fastening the nail that had been driven by the minister, in a sure place" is the challenge of the music leader in selection of the invitational song. It is his job to make sure whether a guest, member, choir, or congregation sings the invitational number that it is salvation "decision-driven."

The choice of songs for the entire service should be prayerfully selected. Unfortunately, this is not always done. Too often a song leader feverishly selects these songs moments before a service is to begin! Phil Kerr stated, "A preacher who perfunctorily delivered a half-hearted sermon would be severely condemned, and rightly so, and yet it is just as important that the musical portion of a service be as wholeheartedly presented as the sermon. There should be as much prayer behind the song service as behind the sermon." (Kerr, 89)

"A revival demands a different type of music. We must have gospel music that will produce results — evangelistic results; gospel music that will turn sinners to God and eternal life." (Matthews, 64)

The choice in music leaders for the revival can either be an asset or deficit. The revival leader ought to be a person who has a passion in evangelism, knowledge of music, charisma of personality, understanding of the proper type music best suited for revival and one who possesses a cooperative attitude. Evangelists and the State Evangelism Department certainly can give assistance in the selection of a revival music leader.

Prelude Music

This music should begin at least five minutes prior to the revival service and be lively, more celebrative in nature as opposed to meditative.

Congregational Music

The music leader must be punctual. The service should start on time. The first word the people hear in the service ought to be from the revival choir or worship team.

Vibrant and "up tempo" hymns/songs that build toward the sermon should be sung. Most hymnals have such songs listed in its topical index under "Evangelism or Salvation." Songs like "Love Lifted Me," "Since Jesus Came into My Heart," "He Keeps Me Singing," "At Calvary," "Only Trust Him," "Whosoever Meaneth Me,"

"Because He Lives," and "Victory in Jesus" all are great revival songs. Revival is not the time to teach a new song unless it is the theme song.

Special Music

Choirs and soloists can add or take away from the service. It all depends on the selection of the song and manner in which it is presented. My experience has taught me that the music director should not assume the guest singer(s) know their time allotment and should specifically inform them they have six minutes on the program. This is sufficient time for them to sing two selections if they refrain from talking. Effective singers with rare exceptions allow their music to do the preaching. The music director and audio engineer must be responsible for making sure that any tape or CD a guest singer requires is cued and ready to play. In addition to the distraction un-cued music creates, spiritual momentum is hindered. Revival musicians and singers should be 'tried and proven'. Revival is not the time to 'showcase' the untrained or ungifted.

Special music should be sung during the offertory. The choir or singer(s) need to be ready to sing without delay the moment the offertory prayer is concluded.

Nothing is more distracting and distasteful then musicians or singers departing the service after their part on the program. Make it a fast-clad rule that if a music guest cannot attend the entire service they cannot participate on the program.

Invitational Music

The invitation must tie in with the sermon without any break or delay. I like for the musician to get in place while I am praying at the end of my message and begin playing the invitational song quietly. I instruct them that I always have a prayer at the close of my message during which time I would like for them to move to the instrument and begin playing softly "Just As I Am." I tell the crusade/revival song leader that I will announce the invitational hymn and will indicate to him by hand or facial gesture at what point he is to lead the congregation or the choir in singing. It is important in my opinion that verbal communication to him is addressed through what is shared in my invitational appeal. For example, I may say, "In just a moment the choir will sing, and you will have an opportunity to make a life-changing decision." Hearing that, the song leader knows when I finish that appeal the choir should be ready immediately to begin singing.

Too many great evangelistic sermons have been quenched by musician distraction as they get up and move to their instrument. The invitation must flow without interruption straight from the sermon. Avoid "dead spots" between the sermon and the invitation.

The invitational song is all-important and should be selected in consultation with the revival evangelist. This gives assurance that the song will fit with the message preached and be a spiritual hammer to further drive its point home. This teamwork is essential for the invitational to flow smoothly and effectively. The invitation is not the time to teach a new song to the congregation. The song selected should be one that people can sing without difficulty, allowing their minds to churn over the decision the minister is inviting them to make. By all means, the lyrics of the invitation hymn should be theologically sound. Preferably the invitational song should be printed for distribution as the service begins or projected onto a large screen as the invitation begins. This prevents distractions that can result from getting hymnals out of the rack, the announcement of hymn numbers, and the rustling of turning pages to get to the number selected. Another possibility is having the music minister prior to the message to ask the congregation to insert their bulletin in the hymnal at the invitation hymn; when the time to sing comes, the page is already marked and an announcement does not have to be made.

Particularly effective evangelistic invitational hymns:
Just as I Am
I Have Decided To Follow Jesus
The Savior Is Waiting
Pass Me Not, O Gentle Savior
Only Trust Him
Softly and Tenderly
Almost Persuaded
His Way With Thee
Why Do You Wait
Take My Life and Let It Be
Christ Receiveth Sinful Men
Have Thine Own Way
I Am Resolved
Jesus, I Come • Lord, I'm Coming Home
His Way With Thee • Jesus Is Lord Of All
I Surrender All • Almost Persuaded

Particularly effective evangelistic invitational choruses:
I Will Never Be The Same Again
Wonderful, Merciful Savior
More Love, More Power
Open The Eyes Of My Heart, Lord
There Is A Redeemer
Change My Heart, O God

Particularly effective evangelistic invitational contemporary solo songs:
Come, Just As You Are
Holiness (Take My Life)
We Fall Down
You Are My King (Amazing Love)
Draw Me Close
Knowing You
Five Rows Back
All Who Are Thirsty
The Power of Your Love
Above All
The Wonderful Cross

Particularly effective evangelistic invitational choir anthems:
Eagles Wings
You Alone
Purified
Draw Me Close to You
Bow the Knee
The Potter's Hand
Changed

Particularly effective evangelistic invitational traditional solos:
I'd Rather Have Jesus
Have You Any Room For Jesus?
A Hill Called Mount Calvary
Do You Know My Jesus?
Face To Face With Christ My Savior
Without Him
People Need the Lord
Amazing Grace
The King is Coming
The Old Rugged Cross Made the Difference
The Old Rugged Cross
The Midnight Cry

Closing Music

I like for a revival service to end with a victory chorus or hymn refrain like that of "Victory in Jesus" or "Awesome God." This brief song should be ready to be sung immediately following the benedictory prayer of the pastor or in place of it.

Chapter Five
The Publicity in Revival

The devil comes along with something the natural man wants, and he paints the town red to let them know he is coming. The church comes along with something the natural man doesn't want, and thousands of pastors seem to think a mere announcement of the project from the pulpit is quite enough. —W. E. Biederwolf (Autry, 109)

The obvious purpose for publicity of the revival meeting is to inform the church and community of its date and time, prompting their attendance. It is not to preach the gospel. John Bisagno cautioned, "Revival publicity should not be overbearing in its religious zeal. To say, 'Are you tired of sin? Try Christ, Find new life in Jesus,' is to preach to them. Don't give them the plan of salvation in your publicity. Advertise the preacher and the team. Then, when the people come to hear, it will be the team's job to point them to the Christ." (Bisagno, 57-58)

In advertising, state as pointedly as possible the who, what, when and where of the revival. "Through efficient publicity, the church is able to get the attention of the world and to create a desire on the part of the people to come to the church to hear the gospel." (Autry, 108)

1. **Newspapers**

Three weeks before the revival, place advertisements in the local newspaper. These announcements should concisely state pertinent details of the revival such as the date, time, and place of the revival and evangelist's identity with photo. Utilize free advertising the newspaper may give in their religious section and purchase advertising for choice spots in sections read by more that are un-churched and unsaved.

NEWS RELEASE

The_____Church

located at _____

in _____will host Revival Services Sunday morning,

_____ (date) through Wednesday evening,

_____ (date) with Evangelist Shivers.

    Rev. Shivers is in his thirty-fourth year as the full-time preaching evangelist of the Frank Shivers Evangelistic Association, Columbia, SC. He has authored nine books the latest of which is entitled Revivals 101. Rev. Shivers is also the director of Longridge Camp and Retreat Center, Ridgeway, South Carolina, which has ministered to students for the past twenty-seven years. He is a member of both the State and National Conference of Southern Baptist Evangelists.

    The Sunday morning service will be at 11:00 while the evening services are scheduled for 7:00. Special singing will be provided each service and nursery services will be available. Pastor _____

and the members of _____

invite you to come and share in these special services with them. Please call

_____ if more information is needed.

---

2. **Television and Radio**

    Check with local cable television providers and radio stations with regard to free spots. Keep these short and to the point.

3. **Flyers, Window Posters, Placards, Bumper Stickers, Door Knob Hangers**

    As an evangelist for over three decades, I can say resolutely that "home-spun" publicity in black and white often gives an impression the church doesn't realize and fails to maximize the intended purposes. Color printing used to be cost prohibitive but no longer. Consult and contract with a printer professional to publish all revival material. A graphic designer expertly could prepare layouts for all revival publicity with continuity. Doing it right will be costly, but it will return positive dividends that will long outlast the days of revival.

4. **Yard Signs**

    Hundreds of free advertisements can be utilized in having members of the church place a yard sign on their property that might read "SOLD ON REVIVAL. Calvary Baptist Church, October 10 – 13, 7:00 p.m."

5. **Email**

   Encourage church members to email everyone in their email address book with an invitation to attend the revival. Include in this invitation a request to forward the email to others.

6. **Billboards**

   Billboard advertising on a busy thoroughfare is invaluable but often cost prohibitive. Companies renting billboard advertising may be willing to reduce its fee to the church for revival promotion.

7. **Telephone**

   Enlist members to call everyone in the phone directory two days prior to the revival inviting them to attend. Divide the phone directory into sections of 25 names and distribute to willing callers.

8. **Pastoral Letters**

   A letter from the pastor or evangelist inviting both members and prospects to attend the revival should be mailed one week prior to the revival.

9. **Mass Mailing**

   A mass mailing targeting the zip-code(s) of the church's ministry field promoting the revival should have a delivery date no sooner than one week prior to the revival.

What Influences People to Salvation

Advertisement 2%

Organized Visitation 6%

Contact by Pastor 6%

Friends and Relatives 86%

(Towns, 6)

Chapter Six
The Promotion in Revival

An obstetrician cannot deliver physical life until there has been conception and a period of gestation. This is also true of the "spiritual obstetrician," the evangelist."
—*Sterling Huston* (Douglas, Calling of An Evangelist, 235)

"With all our activity and preparing, with all our longing and praying, we dare not forget that revival is the sovereign work of an all-powerful God. The church cannot demand it, plan it, or control it; it is God's to give and to order." (Edward, 239)

Publicity announces the revival. Promotion attracts to revival. I have witnessed about every kind of promotion that can be offered in a revival including a young seminary pastor's pledge to house and feed a goat for a week if a certain number attended. What amazed me with that promotion is it worked. I know because I was that young pastor! As long as they are in good taste, effective, and do not demean the cause of Christ, promotions should be prayerfully considered. I will share five extremely effective promotions. (No goats!)

1. **Youth Night at Revival**

Youth night by far has been the most effective promotion I have seen utilized. This promotion involves students receiving free tickets to distribute to friends to attend a Pizza Blast being held an hour prior to the revival service. Students attending the Pizza Blast understand they are to stay for the youth night service. The program for the Pizza Blast pre-service should be casual and complete with games and a brief evangelistic presentation from the evangelist. Cards and pencils should be available to register all who attend. A time frame of one hour is ample for this event.

As an added incentive to get students to attend announce there will be a drawing for valuable prizes. You may publicize a few of the biggest ones.

Pizza Blast tickets may be prepared "in house." Include the time and date of the event along with the time frame (example: 6:00 – 8:15 p.m.). It may be helpful to include a phone number for transportation (if the church is able to make pick-ups). In a noticeable manner, the ticket should indicate that the ticket must be presented to gain entrance to the Pizza Blast. This promotion is most effective on a school night; students have opportunities at school to pump classmates to attend during the day. The evangelist in the main service should speak on a topic relevant to youth.

PIZZA BLAST ADMISSION TICKET
Ticket must be presented at the Door for Admission
6:00 – 8:15 p.m.*   Tuesday, March 5
First Baptist Church Fellowship Hall
3333 Calvary Street
Transportation Call 888-0000
*Includes a Youth Service at 7:00 p.m.

---

2. **Children Night at Revival**
   Similar to the youth night promotion, except instead of a Pizza Blast host a Hot Dog Supper (without the chili) for children. A 45 minute time frame is ample for this event. Prepare tickets for children to distribute (adapt Youth Pizza Blast ticket). Invite the guest evangelist to share briefly with the children a simple evangelistic message prior to their departure to the sanctuary for the main service. It is important that adults sit with the children in the night service.
3. **Sunday School Night at Revival**
   This promotion enlists each Sunday School Teacher to the task of getting 100 percent of their class to attend a specified night during revival. Each teacher endeavors to accomplish this goal by having members sign pledge cards of their intent to attend and through reminding members of this special night by cards, email and phone calls. Reserved seating in the sanctuary must be marked for each class with banners or posters. Each teacher should be recognized and presented with a study help that will enhance their teaching.
4. **Pack-a-Pew Night**
   This promotion works when it is well organized but fails miserably when it is not. Announcing the promotion of a pack-a-pew night without assigning pew captains never ever works. I know. I have witnessed it. This is one promotion best not used if not used

right. Assign pew captains to be responsible for filling every pew in the church. In cases where the pews are extra long, it may be necessary to assign two captains. Urge these captains to enlist not only church members but prospects to sit on their pew. Award the winning captain with a study resource.

Place a large diagram of the sanctuary pews complete with pew captains cited for each in the foyer of the church.

5. **Operation Andrew**

Operation Andrew is based on soul cultivation of the unsaved with the explicit purpose to have them attend an evangelistic service. The Billy Graham Evangelistic Association has utilized this approach in their crusades for years with great effectiveness.

Operation Andrew is a single, five step plan.

Operation Andrew

"Andrew first findeth his own brother Peter ... and he brought him to Jesus." (John 1:41-42)

1. ***Look Around***

List the names of ten unsaved people in your 'circle' or beyond.

2. **Look Up**

Pray daily for each person on your list and look for opportunities to express God's love to them.

3. **Look Out**

Discover ways to cultivate friendships and create trust with each person on your list.

4. **Look Forward**

Invite each person on your list to attend a revival service with you; a night that the service will be evangelistic in nature.

5. **Look After**

Encourage those from your list that get saved. Don't give up on those from your list that do not.

My Operation Andrew List

1. _____

2. _____

3. _____

4. _____

5. _____

6. _____

7. _____

8. _____

9. _____

10. _____

Sterling Huston stated, "Sowing is indispensable in the preparation for evangelism if we expect to reap souls. (I Corinthians 3:6) The gift of an evangelist is effective only as other gifts of the church are exercised. Christians must sow the good seed of the Word through their witness, and water it with loving concern and prayer, to prepare the harvest for the work of the evangelist." (Douglas, Calling of An Evangelist, 235)

Operation Andrew can be promoted for one or more special nights in the revival along with other special night emphasis.

"The greatest discovery about evangelistic preaching is that it requires the members to be partners of the minister. The finest sermons will move nothing but the air unless someone has been brought to hear them, and that is what the laity are best equipped to do." (Sweazey,167) The key to success in a revival, crusade or Harvest Day is doing the hundred of hours of community visitation and cultivation inviting the unsaved and church member prospect to attend. This endeavor without question requires church wide support.

Ten Surprises About the Unchurched

Surprise No. 1
Most of the unchurched prefer to attend church on Sunday morning if they attend.

Surprise No. 2
Most of the unchurched feel guilty about not attending church.

Surprise No. 3
Ninety-six percent of the unchurched are at least somewhat likely to attend church if they are invited.

Surprise No. 4
Very few of the unchurched had someone share with them how to become a Christian.

Surprise No. 5
Most of the unchurched have a positive view of pastors, ministers and the church.

Surprise No. 6
Many of the unchurched have a church background.

Surprise No. 7
Some types of "cold calls" are effective; many are not. The definition of "cold call" is simply "uninvited." The type of cold-call evangelism most often resisted by the unchurched is an uninvited visit to their homes.

Surprise No. 8
The unchurched would like to develop a real and sincere relationship with a Christian.

Surprise No. 9
The attitudes of the unchurched are not correlated to where they live, their ethnic or racial background, or their gender.

Surprise No. 10
Many of the unchurched are far more concerned about the spiritual well-being of their children than themselves.
(Rainer, "the unchurched next door", 23-29)

There are many more special night promotions the church may utilize such as "Bring a Friend night," "Family night," "Deacon Family Ministry night," "Music night," and "Call the Church Roll night," but these that I have noted have a proven track record in my ministry.

It is most imperative the pastor promote the special emphasizes of the nightly revival services with enthusiasm and expectancy. I suggest the following scheduling.

Sunday Night	Pack a Pew Night
Monday Night	Sunday School Night/Operation Andrew
Tuesday Night	Youth Night
Wednesday Night	Children Night

Additionally a "SonRise" youth service may be scheduled the last thirty minutes of Sunday School the start of revival. Youth are gathered in an assembly room to hear the evangelist share a gospel presentation and be challenged to bring friends to the Pizza Blast on the scheduled night.

Charles Finney states, "I said that a revival is the result of the right use of the appropriate means. The means which God has enjoined for the production of a revival doubtless have a natural tendency to produce a revival. Otherwise God would not have enjoined them. But means will not produce a revival, we all know, without the blessing of God. No more will grain, when it is sown, produce a crop without the blessing of God. It is impossible for us to say that there is not as direct an influence or agency from God, to produce a crop of grain, as there is to produce a revival. What are the laws of nature according to which it is supposed that grain yields a crop? They are nothing but the constituted manner of the operations of God. In the Bible, the Word of God is compared to grain, and preaching is compared to sowing the seed, and the results to the springing up and growth of the crop. A revival is as naturally a result of the use of the appropriate means as a crop is of the use of its appropriate means." (Finney)

I know of two high school students due to a promotion by an evangelist were responsible for 105 'guests' in a revival service. I know this to be true for I was one of those teens. In case you are curious I won the Bible having 53 guests in attendance. A promotion indeed worked in my case and will in the lives of others if properly handled.

> "If we find a revival that is not spoken against, we had better look again to ensure that it is a revival." Arthur Wallis (Edwards, 221)

Chapter Seven
The Preparation in Revival

Someone has said there can be no Pentecost without Plenty
Cost.   —*E.J. Daniels* (Daniels, 6)

Revival has two parts: ours and God's. The church's part according to 2 Chronicles 7:14 is to prepare and God's part is to provide; ours to seek it and His to send it. God's part is contingent upon the church doing its part. He has ordained "revival fire" to be ignited upon this condition. The church's part apart from God's part would be most futile. The church must work and prepare for revival as if all depended upon her but then rely upon God as if all depended upon Him for it does. "All is vain unless the Spirit of the Holy One comes down; Brethren, pray and holy manna will be showered all around." Billy Graham stated, "I believe that God is true to His Word, and that He must rain righteousness upon us if we meet His conditions." (Drummond, <u>Canvas Cathedral</u>, 426)

The revival at Mt. Carmel illustrates this point. (I Kings 18: 17 – 39) To expose Baal as a false god and Jehovah as the true and living God, the prophet Elijah made ready a sacrifice. This sacrifice required preparation. "The altar of the Lord that was broken down" had to be repaired (v 30); the bullock had to be flayed and placed on the wood (v 33); and a trench had to be made to encircle the altar (v 32). Elijah thus led the people to do their part for the fire of God to fall. Next Elijah ordered four barrels of water to be poured "on the burnt sacrifice and on the wood" not once, or twice but three times to the end that "the water ran round about the altar" (v 33) and then he "filled the trench also with water" (v34) to make clear that when the fire consumed the sacrifice it was solely the hand of God. Elijah prayed for God to send the Fire, which He did and revival broke out to the degree the people "Fell on their faces: and they said, The Lord, he is the God; the Lord, he is the God." (v 38 – 39) The church must do its part in preparation for revival and then pour water upon it making clear it is God who sends the "Holy Fire."

James Burns cautioned, "Revivals do not come by caprice because the church does certain things in a formal, structured fashion.

Although the people of God have their part, the sovereignty of God stands central in real revival." (Drummond, <u>Canvas Cathedral</u>, 418)

In reference to church revival, Curtis Hutson stated, "The reason many things do not work is that the average congregation already has an idea of what they think will work and what they think will not work, and they accept only the part they have already agreed upon. If the pastor or evangelist happens to give something contrary to what they believe or think, they are not willing to try it." (Hutson, 96) The pastor must be open-minded and lead his people to be likewise regarding the implementation of a revival preparation plan.

Intense and thorough preparation is imperative if the church is to have the "Fire of Heaven" fall in sweeping revival. Preparation separates "meetings" from "revivals". The more people the pastor can get involved in preparing for revival, the greater will be its attendance and success. It is advisable to form eight committees to work under the pastor's leadership to assist in planning the revival. Committees ought to be comprised of members gifted or talented if possible in the field they are to serve. The size of each committee is dependent upon the workload required. All committees are to meet for organizational purposes five weeks prior to the revival to form a countdown calendar for their work. It is essential that a deadline for each committee to complete its task is set by the pastor. Additionally the pastor should schedule on the master revival countdown calendar weekly meetings with the revival committees for progress reports. The pastor in his selection of each committee names its chairperson. Once the committees are in place, the pastor's responsibility primarily is to monitor their work and assure that their assignment is done properly and timely.

1. **Publicity Committee**

This committee publicizes the revival through the means detailed in Chapter Four.

2. **Promotion Committee**

This committee is responsible for the promotion and execution of each nightly emphasis in the revival except Sunday School Night and *Operation Andrew*. Members of this committee are responsible for printing tickets, ordering and serving pizza and hot dogs, and preparing the diagram of the sanctuary for pack-a-pew night. Due to the manifold task of this committee, it should have at least seven members.

3. **Prayer Committee**

This committee enlists members to pray for the revival through hosting cottage prayer meetings, 24-hour prayer vigils, and providing "reminder to pray" prayer tents.

The "prayer tent" should have printed on one side the information below and on the other side the date and time of the revival, as well as a photo of the evangelist. Members are encouraged to place this "prayer tent" upon their dining room table as a reminder to pray for revival at meal times.

PRAY FOR REVIVAL

Pray for the Speaker
- Soul and Study preparation
- Sermon preparation
- Sensitivity of and Submission to the guidance of the Holy Spirit
- Safety in his travel and from sickness
- Supernatural Strength for preaching and in Soulwinning
- Staunch reliance in the Sufficiency of Jesus Christ to use him mightily
- Separation from Sin and Steadfastness in Truth
- Shielding from distraction, discouragement, deception and doubt

Pray for the Saint
- Recognize the need for Revival
- Remove every hindrance from attending the Revival
- Repentance of and Renunciation of personal sin
- Reception of and Response to the gospel preached
- Relentless effort to invite the unsaved to attend the services
- Resignation to pray fervently and continuously for the evangelist, others and themselves until the fire of revival falls
- Resolve to expect great things from God and to attempt great things for God

Pray for the Sinner
- Cultivation by Christian friends urging their attendance at the revival
- Concern for their own soul that prompts attendance at the revival
- Concentration upon the Gospel that is proclaimed
- Conviction of sin, judgment and righteousness and need of a Savior
- Conversion through faith and repentance in Jesus Christ
- Conservation by saints that enable their growth in Godliness

"If my people, which are called by my name, shall humble themselves, and pray, and seek my face and turn from their wicked ways; then will I hear from heaven, and will forgive their sin, and will heal their land." (2 Chronicles 7:14)

T.A. Hegre said, "If the church would only awaken to her responsibly of intercession, we could well evangelize the world in short time." (Ravenhill, 13) R. A. Torrey declared, "It is doubtful if even a single soul is born again without travail of soul on the part of someone." (Barlow) Leonard Ravenhill wrote, "The prayer chamber is a mirror reflecting our spiritual condition." (Ravenhill, 139)

Alvin I. Reid told of a picture in a pastor's study of a man prostrate on the floor praying. The caption, in large letters declared, MAKE WAR ON THE FLOOR. (Reid, 51) The church must make war on the floor in prayer for the unsaved, that they may be enlightened to the Truth of Christ, and for his soul, that he will see the need of Christ and alter his will so that he will say yes to Christ. Prayer blasts satanic strongholds in the sinner's life granting deliverance from the blindness of the flesh, the pride of life and the shackles of sin (2 Corinthians 10:4). Likewise the church must fervently pray for renewal among the cold, casual, and carnal saint. Sidlow Baxter stated, "Men may spurn our appeals, reject our message, oppose our arguments, despise our persons, but they are helpless against our prayers."

C.H. Spurgeon stated, "Christian men should never speak of 'getting up a revival.' Where are you going to get it *up* from? I do not know any place from which you can get it *up*. We must bring revival *down* if it is to be worth having. We must enquire of the Lord to do it for us. Too often the temptation is to enquire for an eminent revivalist, or ask whether a great preacher could be induced to come. Now, I do not object to inviting soul-winning preachers, or to any other plans of usefulness, but our main business is to enquire of the Lord, for after all, He alone can give the increase." (Edwards, 239)

4. **The Counseling Committee**

This committee consists of men and women who are experienced soulwinners who will serve as counselors during the invitation in the revival services. The pastor should review with this committee the plan of salvation and personal renewal with instruction concerning witnessing at the altar. No person should be allowed to counsel in the revival who has not met with the pastor.

Counseling at the Altar

Trained counselors must be prepared to give assistance during the evangelist's invitational appeal at the conclusion of a sermon for decisions of salvation; church membership; baptism and personal renewal. The following is a general preparatory counselor guide for all decisions but here adapted specifically to the decision of salvation. I suggest the use of Campus Crusade's *Have You Made The Wonderful Discovery Of The Spirit-Filled Life?* for decisions of renewal.

1. Readiness.

The counselor's Bible and witnessing plan must be in his possession during each service. The counselor should anticipate being called upon for assistance during every invitation.

2. Prayerfulness.

Let the counselor pray prior to the invitation, "O Lord, please grant others and me the high privilege to lead some soul to saving grace during the invitation. Move upon the sinner's heart with convicting power, remove every obstacle in his way to salvation, and grant him courage to respond publicly."

3. Watchfulness.

The counselor ought to be seated on the front pew during the invitation for quick and easy access by the minister. During the invitation he must be alert to the minister's signal for needed assistance which may be communicated through eye contact, a nod, or tap on the shoulder.

4. Introduction.

The minister should always briefly introduce the counselor to the prospect by saying, "John, this is Billy Smith, one of our counselors. He will explain to you more about what is involved in becoming a Christian." Counselors will be paired with "seekers" of their own gender.

5. Presentation.

A lengthy gospel presentation is not necessary in most cases due to the message the prospect just heard. A review of the basics of salvation should conclude with the counselor saying, "Would you like to pray with me to receive Jesus Christ into your life as Lord and Savior?" Upon a yes response, the soul winner should lead the sinner in the sinner's prayer and give assurance that Jesus keeps His promise to save all who call upon Him in faith and repentance.

6. Direction.

The counselor should encourage the new convert to make a decision about baptism and church membership.

7. Follow-Up.

The counselor should place in the hands of the new believer a copy of "*What to do Now?*" or some other simple and concise follow up booklet that details the first steps of the Christian life.

8. Information.

A decision card must be completed by the counselor for each person he presents the gospel. This record should be hand printed for clarity.

9. Communication.

The counselor upon returning to the sanctuary with the new believer should sit on the front pew. At this point the counselor should wait for the right moment to communicate this decision to the minister.

10. Trouble Shooting.

There always should be a designated trained counselor available during the invitation to give any necessary assistance to the soul winners around the altar.

5. **The Sunday School Committee**

This committee is comprised of the Sunday School director and secretary. This committee promotes and prepares for Sunday School Night at the revival. These members are responsible for preparing a banner for each class and fastening it to the assigned pew at least 30 minutes prior to the service. In the service the Sunday School director will recognize each teacher and present them with a teaching resource.

6. **The Nursery Committee**

This committee secures outside qualified help in providing nursery services for the revival so that all members may attend each service in the revival, daily inspects the nursery to make sure all is "spic and span," and publicizes the time the nursery will be open and its location. The nursery should be open at least 30 minutes prior to the revival service. This committee should instruct ushers (greeters) to encourage parents to place their child under age four in the nursery.

7. **The Outreach Committee**

This committee promotes prospect visitation and *Operation Andrew*. In *Soulwinning 101,* I share many methods of outreach that this committee can easily implement. "A planned partnership between the minister who brings the message and the members who bring the hearers is the first essential for evangelistic preaching." (Sweazey, 168)

This committee is responsible for enlisting visitation teams, locating prospects, preparing assignment cards, and making visitation assignment. A suggested goal is to secure two visitation teams (two people per team) from each Sunday School class (youth – adult). Visits are to be made the Saturday prior to revival.

8. **The Greeters (usher) Committee**

Cheerful greeters ought to be stationed at each door before and after the services to meet guests and provide assistance. A hearty "Glad you came" and "Please come back" is imperative. Ushers are to re-stack the offering envelopes in the pews prior to each service and receive the love offering at the designated time. Additionally ushers are to encourage parents to place their children four years old and younger in the nursery.

Other committees may be utilized in planning for the revival but these are the most essential.

Keep the Church Calendar clear for revival.
All interfering events or meetings scheduled on the church calendar for the week of revival must be postponed. Once, when leading a revival I discovered that the church softball team was out on the field playing a game as I was preaching!

Pastoral preaching in preparation for revival.
The pastor's preaching on biblical revivals, historical revivals, and prayer will enhance readiness and excitement for revival in the church. Heart Cry for Revival (Stephen Olford), Revivals in the Bible (Ernest Baker), Why Revival Tarries (Leonard Ravenhill), and True Revival and the Men God Uses (Horatius Bonar) are excellent resources on the subject of revival.

C.H. Spurgeon's sermons "The Key to Revival" (Revelation 2: 4-5) and I Kings 18: 42 – 46 and Charles G. Finney's sermon "When Revival is to be Expected" (Psalm 85:6) are illustrative of preparatory sermons for revival.

C.H. Spurgeon's Sermon "The Key to Revival"
(Revelation 2: 4-5)

I. Christ Perceives. Our Lord sorrowfully perceives the faults of His church. "Nevertheless I have somewhat against thee."

II. Christ Prescribes. The Savior's prescription is found in three words. "Remember, Repent, Return."

A. Remember. "Thou hast left thy first love."

B. Repent. "Repent as you did at the first and do thy first works."

C. Return. "Return to thy first deeds at once. In doing the first deeds you will prove that you have come back to your first love."

III. Christ Persuades. The Lord Jesus persuades His erring one to repent.

A. Persuades with a warning. "I will come unto thee and will remove thy candlestick out of its place, except thou repent." The candlestick:

1. Symbolizes the comfort of the Word.

2. Symbolizes usefulness. He can take away from the church her very existence as a church. Ephesus is gone, nothing but ruins can be found. I persuade you from my very soul not to encounter these dangers, not to run these terrible risks; for as you would not wish to see either the church or your own self without God's light, to pine in darkness, it is necessary that you abide in Christ and go on to love Him more and more.

B. Persuades with a promise. "To Him that overcometh will I give to eat of the tree of life, which is in the midst of the paradise of God."

1. Those who lose their first love fall, but those who abide in love are made to stand.

2. Those who lose their first love wander far, but if you keep your first love you shall not wander, but you shall come into closer fellowship. (Backhouse, 140-156)

C.H. Spurgeon's Sermon on I Kings 18:42-46.

C.H. Spurgeon used I Kings 18:44 to illustrate the small signs (clouds) that precede revival. As Elijah was praying for rain on Mt. Carmel he "said to his servant, 'Go up now, look toward the sea.' And he went up, and looked, and said, 'There is nothing.' And he said, 'Go again seven times.'" (v 43) On the seventh time the servant reported, "Behold, there ariseth a little cloud out of the sea, like a man's hand." (v 44) Spurgeon shared four "certain signs and tokens for good which prayerful faith clearly perceives when an awakening, a genuine revival is about to come." Consider the "small clouds" the size of a man's hand that surface when God is about to do a mighty work.

1. A growing dissatisfaction with the present state of things, and an increasing anxiety among the members of the church for the salvation of souls.

2. When this anxiety leads believers to be exceedingly earnest and importunate in prayer.

3. When ministers begin to take counsel one with another, and to say, "What must we do?"

4. When we shall see the doctrine of the individual responsibility of each Christian fully felt and carried out into individual action.

Charles G. Finney's Sermon "When Revival is to be Expected"
(Psalm 85:6)

Finney in this sermon has four main points, one of which I will detail.

A. A revival may be expected when the providence of God indicates that a revival is at hand. There is a conspiring of events to open the way, a preparation of circumstances to favor a revival, so that those who are looking for it can see that a revival is at hand just as plainly as if it had been revealed from Heaven. There are various ways for God to indicate His will to a people – sometimes by giving them peculiar means, sometimes by peculiar and alarming events, sometimes by remarkably favoring the employment of means, such as by the weather, health and so on.

B. A revival may be expected when the wickedness of the wicked grieves and humbles and distresses Christians.

C. A revival may be expected when Christians have a spirit of prayer for a revival – that is, when they pray as if their hearts were set upon a revival.

D. A revival may be expected when the attention of ministers is especially directed to this particular object and when their preaching and other efforts are aimed particularly at the conversion of sinners.

E. A revival may be expected when Christians begin to confess their sins to one another. At other times, they confess in a general manner, as if they were only half in earnest.

F. A revival may be expected whenever Christians are found willing to make the sacrifice necessary to carry it on. They must be willing to sacrifice their feelings, their business, their time, to help forward the work.

G. A revival may be expected when ministers and professors are willing to have God promote it by what instruments He pleases.

H. A revival may be expected when the foregoing things occur. A revival, to the same extent, already exists. In truth, a revival should be *expected* whenever it is *needed.*

Remarks:

1. Do you need revival? Do you expect to have one? Have you any reason to expect one?

2.   You see why you have not revival. It is only because you do not want one, because you are not praying for it nor anxious for it nor putting forth efforts for it.

3.   Do you wish for a revival? Will you have one? If God should ask you this moment by an audible voice from Heaven, "Do you want a revival?" would you dare say "Yes"? If He said, "Are you willing to make the sacrifices?" would you answer, "Yes"? If He asked, "When shall it begin?" would you answer, "Let it begin tonight – let it begin here- let it begin in my heart NOW"? Would you dare say so to God if you should hear His voice tonight? (Smith, 125-134)

Dr. R. A. Torrey said, "I can give a prescription that will bring a revival to any church or community or any city on earth. First, let a few Christians (they need not be many) get right with God themselves. This is a prime essential. If this is not done, the rest of what I say will come to nothing. Second, let them bind themselves together in a prayer group to pray for a revival until God opens the heavens and comes down. Third, let them put themselves at the disposal of God, for Him to use as He sees fit in winning others to Christ. That is all!" Torrey said of this prescription for revival, "It cannot fail." The three points of this prescription for revival are "preachable."

Bill Stafford stated, "We will never have revival until we say 'No part dark.'"

Chapter Eight
The Program in Revival

The program for the revival service should fit an hour's time frame. It is surprising how much can be included in a service if all involved stay on task and there is no drag time. A typical revival service includes a choir anthem/theme song, congregational singing, welcome, introductions and prayer, special music, love offering, the sermon, and invitation.

6:55	Musical Prelude
7:00	Choir Anthem/Theme Song
7:05	Congregational Singing (two hymns/praise songs)
7:10	Welcome/Introductions/Prayer
7:13	Special Music
7:17	Offertory hymn/love offering for the evangelist
	Special Music (while offering is received)
7:25	Message
	Decision Hymn
	Departing Praise Chorus

Sunday morning services should follow the same format. Churches that have two Sunday morning services should combine them, space permitting, for a united evangelistic/revival thrust.

My experience has taught that often churches try to squeeze too much singing or announcing or dramatizing or testifying into the revival service. The pastor must jealously guard the revival preacher's time making sure he is in the pulpit no later than 25 to 30 minutes from the start time of the service. He must make sure others on the program know their time allotment and will operate within its limits. As an evangelist I have had pastors in revival services whisper into my ear at 7:45 p.m. or later (based on a 7:00 p.m. start) "Don't worry about the time. Preach as long as you want."

Arising to preach 45 minutes or more into a service handicaps the evangelist and hampers receptivity to his message. In regard to reaching souls, it is profitable to get him in the pulpit "sooner than later." My experience in evangelism has taught me that to exceed the allotted time in a service may (and often does) jeopardize the attendance for the remaining services. Children have school and many adults have work the next morning necessitating a timely dismissal. People are willing to understand the extension of a service due to the movement of the Holy Spirit or invitational response but not that due to prolonged singing or announcements.

Preview testimonials for theological and edifying content as well as structure. Testimonials ought to be shared in a two- to three-minute time frame. "Thank you for salvaging the service," I was told following a revival service in which I had to speak after three testimonials lasted nearly thirty minutes. I had to lay my sermon aside and simply give the invitation. Sadly, evangelists have to "salvage services" too often due to lengthy, unwarranted and unbiblical testifying. With regard to testimonials in revival, a pastor should have the policy, "No preview, no program." Biblically sound and structured testimonials in revival may help, but the opposite certainly will hurt.

Revival praying should be passionate, specific, and concise. D.L. Moody stated, "If you pray three minutes, I'll pray with you. If you pray six minutes, I'll pray for you. If you pray nine minutes, I'll pray against you."

Chapter Nine
The Preacher in Revival

I have used, am using, and will always use the ministry of full-time evangelists.   *—Herb Reavis, Jr.*

Johnny Hunt stated that he uses vocational evangelists for three reasons: "First of all, because the Bible teaches that God has gifted the church with those with the gift of the evangelist. Secondly, I have seen through the years that because of this gift, God uses these men to be able to "draw the net" like no one else. Thirdly, it is because I love the obedience in the life of the men who are willing to give their lives to this faith-based ministry." (Hunt)

Selection of the preacher to lead in revival should be based upon the impression of the Holy Spirit. I have always believed that God is able to put His man of the hour in just the right church if the Holy Spirit is allowed to give guidance. Keep in mind God gifts some to be harvest evangelists primarily and others revivalists. An evangelist working within the realms of his specific giftedness is the most effective. It is crucial to 'fit' the man with the 'task.'

God has endowed some pastors with a special gift of evangelism and revivalism, and these have done a great work in the arena of revival. If I was in the pastorate, I would have such a pastor preach in the spring revival and promote renewal and then have an evangelist preach in the fall meeting and promote evangelism. The church in using a pastor must do diligence regarding his needs.

God has ordained evangelists for His church. (Ephesians 4:11) "It is an office which has always been of great importance in the Church. It is much needed today. While almost any preacher can learn how to be effective in evangelism, there are some who have a rare genius for it. Specialists develop skills which God can greatly use." (Sweazey, 166). D.L. Moody commented on Ephesians 4:11 by stating, "Dead men need evangelists. Living men need pastors and teachers. Evangelists are quarrymen who dig out the stone. Pastors are stonecutters who take off the rough edges. Teachers are those who put them in place!" Some pastors say, "We can't afford an evangelist" but the church according to scripture cannot afford not to use the evangelist for he is God's gift to the church as a harvester of souls.

Herb Reavis, Jr., stated, "Evangelists are God's gift to the local church." Ephesians 4:11 says, "And He Himself gave some to be …evangelists…" It was a Southern Baptist evangelist who taught me how to lead someone to Christ when I was just starting out in ministry. The greatest spiritual harvests I have experienced in the churches I have served have happened under the ministry of a full-time vocational evangelist. I have used, am using and will always use the ministry of full-time evangelists." (Reavis)

The Care of the Evangelist

The church is responsible for the protection of, provision for, and prayer on behalf of the evangelist.

Protection. The climate of the day necessitates that evangelists be housed in a motel. Uninterrupted time for prayer, study and sleep is a must, and this setting best serves this need. It is my ministry's policy that I stay in a motel.

Provision. The Apostle Paul declared, "Even so hath the Lord ordained that they which preach the gospel should live of the gospel." The evangelist by faith trusts the church he serves to care for his expenses and financial needs. The expense of owning and driving a vehicle has skyrocketed in the past few years. Churches ought to reimburse the evangelist for expenses incurred with his travel to and from the church. The IRS allowable cost per mile for travel should be the standard. Additionally, the evangelist's meal expense incurred for the total ministry with a church should be reimbursed. It is expedient to contact the evangelist regarding meal preferences. The preference of some evangelists (mine included) is to take meals in a restaurant at their leisure with the pastor and/or businessmen.

The vocational evangelist is not supported by a denomination or agency. He is not paid a salary from a church. He is totally dependent upon the churches he serves to provide for his family and ministry. Out of every dollar that is received in an love offering, a portion must go for annuity, health care, car payment, car insurance, life insurance, house payment, utilities, food, clothing and taxes. The evangelist is not able to minister in revival 52 weeks a year and this necessitates the need of "second-mile offerings." "Second-mile offerings" are those that the people give that exceed the present need of the evangelist for his services.

How can a worthy offering for the evangelist be received? The success of the love offering is largely dependent upon the pastor's attitude in promoting and receiving it. "One of the most common mistakes made in receiving the love offerings, or any type of offering for that matter, is to presume that we must protect the people's pocketbook by not trying very hard. If you make up your mind to get a good offering, one that will be a true expression of love and a blessing to the recipient, then ask for it positively, prayerfully, and with great anticipation. The people will protect their own pocketbooks. If you do it negatively, the people, the evangelist, and the Lord will be embarrassed." (Bisagno, 39) The pastor must make crystal clear the recipient of the love offering each time it is received. The pastor must make sure that all that was received in the offering goes to the evangelist. Thievery is committed by the church when it keeps a portion of the offering designated for the evangelist. It is up to the pastor to prevent this from happening. I have experienced church thievery as has many other evangelists. It is both sad and shocking to read *Churches, Camps and Conference Centers That are Thieves, Rogues, And Rip-off Artists* by Ralph Sexton, Sr. which details the thievery a number of evangelists have experienced at the hands of the church.

How to Receive a Love Offering

1. Prayerfully. Pastor and church should pray for utmost generosity in providing for the needs of God's servant.
2. Personally. The pastor both gives the appeal to contribute and sets the example by giving. Sheep follow the example of the Shepherd.
3. Positively. Confidently and without reservation ask for the people to support the evangelist and his ministry.
4. Persuasively. The pew will take its clue from the pulpit regarding giving.

5. Progressively. Share new information about the evangelist's ministry and his needs prior to each offering.
6. Pointedly. The pastoral offering appeal is to be concise yet unhurried.
7. Promptly. The honorarium/love offering should be disbursed to the evangelist at the conclusion of the revival.

Revival offering envelopes should be stacked at the end of each pew by the ushers prior to the services. During the offertory appeal, the pastor should instruct the person seated nearest the envelopes to take one and pass the others down the pew row.

In addition to the nightly love offering, the church should give the evangelist a budgeted honorarium. I assure you there is no danger that a church will give an evangelist too much! In thirty- four years of evangelism I can attest that the needs of my ministry have seldom been met much less exceeded. I'm confident this is true with most evangelists.

Churches with small memberships can prepare in advance of the revival for the financial need of the evangelist. One church in which I served began receiving love offerings weeks prior to the revival. This offering combined with the offering received during the revival supplied my need. It was obvious that, though numerically small, this church had a big heart and *planned* to supply my need.

In another revival the pastor in my presence challenged several businessmen to make up for the poor offering that had been received. This they did.

I don't know an evangelist that would not be greatly appreciative of even an inadequate love offering in a revival if the people "did what they could." The evangelist's heart is crushed when the offering is inadequate when the people could have done better but simply didn't.

Adopt an evangelist as a church family pledging consistent prayer and financial support. The evangelist and his work will be strengthened by the praying and enabled by the giving. Associations should consider *adopting an evangelist* in the same manner.

Prayer.

Pray for the evangelist, his family and ministry. Pray for the safety of his wife (if married) and children (should he have children) while he ministers in your church. Pray for the evangelist's preparation before and during the revival to preach God's Word. Pray for the Holy Spirit's anointing upon him as he ministers in your church. Pray his health will be maintained, that no sickness or accident will touch him. Pray that his ministry will expand greatly and that his "coast be enlarged." The evangelist begs for the prayers of the church.

The God-called evangelist goes where and when invited without regard to cost or consequence whether he abounds or suffers and whether he is criticized or commended for the sake of lost souls and the glory of God.

Chapter Ten
The Postscript in Revival

"The second half of evangelism is less exciting than the first. Getting decisions is thrilling. It is like a game that can be scored. The results come rapidly, but bringing those decisions to fulfillment in an established Christian life is not very dramatic. It takes months instead of minutes." —*George Sweazey* (Sweazey, 216)

Follow-up or Foul-up. It is estimated that over 50 percent of those who respond affirmatively to a gospel presentation cannot be found in a church service two years later! Discipleship training is not optional but imperative to the conservation of new believers. L. R. Scarborough wrote, "The evangelism that stops at conversion and public profession is lopsided, wasteful, incomplete. It should go on to teach, to train, and to develop, and utilize the talents and powers of the new convert. This educational phase of evangelism is transcendently important." He continued, "Modern evangelism finds here its greatest leakage and waste." (Scarborough, 107-108)

In order to conserve new converts reached in revival, several things are essential.

1. Affirmation

In the follow up visit ask the new believer, "What decision did you make this week in revival?" Let the new convert's lips testify of what happened rather than yours.

2. Adoption

Assign a Barnabas to "adopt" the convert. The Apostle Paul would not have become what he was for God had it not been for Barnabas in his early life. Barnabas took Paul, while just a babe in Christ, under his wings and developed him in the things of Christ. Of this, Luke wrote, "But Barnabas took him (Paul) and brought him to the apostles, and declared unto them how he had seen the Lord in the way, and that he had spoken to him, and how he had preached boldly at Damascus in the name of Jesus" (Acts 9:27). The words "took him" literally mean that Barnabas physically held on to Paul to help him. It is important that every new convert be assigned a Barnabas to "hold on to them" by supplying love, guidance, and protection from spiritual harm. This assignment should be made at the end of the evangelistic service right away and always man with man and woman with woman. Wiersbe wrote, "The term 'disciples' was the most popular name for the early believers. Being a disciple meant more than being a convert or a church member. 'Apprentice' might be an equivalent term. A disciple attached himself to a teacher, identified with him, learned from him, and lived with him. He learned, not simply by listening, but also by doing." (Wiersbe, 107)

3. **Association**

Instruct the convert about biblical baptism encouraging prompt submission (Matthew 28:19). Baptism is like a "gowning" at a graduation ceremony, which does not confer a degree upon a person but symbolizes the degree that already was earned. Believer's baptism is an outward "gowning" publicly of an inward experience of salvation through faith and repentance in Jesus Christ that has already occurred (Acts 20:21). Immediately upon baptism, if not before, the new Christian must be integrated into his new family through the church's Sunday School, worship services, outreach and social activities.

Jimmy Draper, former president of Life-Way believes there is "a lack of urgency" within Southern Baptist churches to baptize. "I've heard from a number of people across our denomination who say professions of faith are good enough," he said. "They are not teaching the importance of publicly identifying with Jesus through baptism, and they're ignoring His command to baptize His followers." (Florida Baptist Witness)

4. **Acquisition**

Instruct the convert in the Word. Jesus exhorted, ". . .teaching them to observe all things whatsoever I have commanded you" (Matthew 28:20). Enroll the new believers in a *What to do Now* study of belief and practice.

5. **Attestation**

Instruct the convert in witnessing. The work of follow up is never complete until the evangelized becomes an evangel testifying of what the Lord has wrought in his life through faith and repentance. The Apostle Paul told young Timothy, "And the things that thou hast heard of me among many witnesses, the same commit thou to faithful men, who shall be able to teach others also" (II Timothy 2:2). This is known as the "ministry of multiplication" and is God's method to evangelize the world. The disciple is to take what he has learned from his godly mentor (teacher) and share it unashamedly with others. Establish the young believer in the faith. It is a hideous sin against him and God to fail to do so. Don't simply stop with a convert at the end of the revival service.

The Follow-Up on the Almost Persuaded
Follow-up upon the unsaved who attended the revival without being converted is imperative. Every revival has in attendance those who are convicted of sin who will not be converted. Two things must be done in behalf of the "Almost Persuaded." First, the church must pray immediately and incessantly that the seed of the gospel that was sown in their heart will be watered and cultivated until it brings forth conversion. The church must also pray that "the birds of the air" will not snatch the gospel seed away. Second, the church must go and witness personally to these who are "Not far from the Kingdom." A witness in private to the 'Almost Persuaded' may lead them out of simple conviction to genuine conversion. This visit must be within days if not hours of their "gospel touch" in the service. Strike while the iron is hot.

Sermon Seeds for the Sunday after Revival
What Stops Revival
Charles Finney addressed the subject "What Stops Revival" in Lectures on Revival. In this message he states 24 things that can stop revival. This message may be downloaded off the Internet.
What Have I Done? (Jeremiah 8: 5-6)
Israel failed to heed the reproval of God in their "revival meeting." In light of God's call to repentance and restoration no man said, "What have I done?" but all immediately resumed the manner of life lived before the revival. In our revival did you stop long enough to ask "What have I (not others) done?" with the rebuttal and reproof of God? Are your lifestyle and priorities any different now than prior to revival? In this message I specifically want you to ask yourself six questions: What have I done with Salvation? What have I done with Separation? What have I done with Surrender? What have I done

with Stewardship? What have I done with Soulwinning? and What have I done with Spiritual Disciplines (Prayer, the Bible, the Church)? In closing, I ask in light of what you have done with these things, what will you now do? It's not too late to have revival.

Don't Come Down (Nehemiah 6: 1 – 9)
Nehemiah had come down to Jerusalem to rebuild the temple walls and re-establish the worship of God. Things were in ruin, and he went with a weeping heart to do something about it. No more had he put his hand to the task, though, that opposition arose from Sanballat and company seeking to stop the work. To their every effort to get him to "come down" and cease the work he replied, "I am doing a great work so that I cannot come down: why should the work cease, while I leave it, and come down to you." God has done a "Great Work" in and among us this week in revival. Satan now will send his Sanballat's encouraging and tempting us to abandon it, to quit on the new commitments made to God. Each of us must be prepared to answer him with the words of Nehemiah, "I am doing a great work and I will not come down." Don't come down to distraction, don't come down to doubt, don't come down to disagreement, don't come down to discouragement, don't come down to a darling sin, and don't come down to disbelief or disapproval (criticism). In closing, ponder what will happen if we don't come down and the results if we do.

The Yet Undecided   (I Kings 18:21)
Elijah addresses this text to those in the "church" who were the undecided ones. He forcefully exclaimed, "How long shalt ye between two opinions?" Make up your mind what place you will give to God in life. Many here made sincere decisions for Christ in our revival but others did not. This message is simply a call to the "Yet Undecided" to decide for Christ in the area in which He is prompting without further delay.

What Keeps Revival Going (2 Chronicles 7:14)
Meeting the conditions of 2 Chronicles 7:14 brought it; continuation of meeting its conditions will keep it.

Escape For Thy Life (Genesis 19:17)
Revival often ends with some close to decision. This sermon by C.H. Spurgeon provides seed thought for a message urging such to decide

immediately for Christ. A possible adaptation of Spurgeon's outline could be *The Why of Escape, The Way of Escape, and the When of Escape.*

The Lord Himself said to Lot, "Escape for thy life," although the command was sent by one of His chosen messengers. God has His messengers nowadays, and He still sends them short, sharp, urgent, stimulating messages like this, "Escape for thy life." I will...try to plead with every unconverted man or woman whom my message may reach; and this shall be the one burden of my pleading, "Escape for thy life."

1. Notice, first, that there was no safety for Lot where he was. He had to escape the doomed city. Therefore, to you who are unconverted, we can bring no proposals of hope if you stay where you are; we can hold out no hope to you either in this world or in that which is to come. Stay where you are, and you are doomed.

2. According to this message of the angel, if Lot is to be saved he must run for it at all costs: "Escape for thy life." He must leave former comrades. Lot had to leave his former comforts. Lot could not stop to argue; nor must you. If Lot is to be rescued, he must, as men say, put his best foot foremost. Lot must not sit down and take things easy, nor must thou. "Escape for thy life."

3. To conclude, let me remind you that Lot had everything at stake, and therefore the angel said to him, "Escape for thy life." Suppose he had stayed in Sodom; then he would have lost all. He would not have saved his furniture, or his gold or his silver; he would have lost all that he had. Again, if Lot had not fled out of Sodom, he would himself have perished. If thou dost neglect the great salvation and dost die and perish in thy iniquity, man, thou hast lost everything! The worst point about the story is that if Lot had not escaped, he would have perished with the men of Sodom. If you are not converted ...you will as surely perish with the worst of men. He also would have perished after having been warned. O Sirs, O Sirs, if you leave go from this Tabernacle to hell, it shall be hard work for you! If you will perish, I will be clear of your blood." (Spurgeon, <u>Twelve Sermons on Decision</u>)

"If revival is being withheld from us it is because some idol remains still enthroned; because we still insist in placing our reliance in human schemes; because we still refuse to face the unchangeable truth that, 'It is not by might, but by My Spirit.'"

— Jonathan Goforth

Works Cited

Allen and Gregory. "Southern Baptist Preaching Today." Nashville: Broadman Press, 1987.

Autry, C.E. Basic Evangelism. Grand Rapids: Zondervan Publishers, 1959.

Backhouse, Robert, ed. Spurgeon on Revival. Eastbourne: Kingsways Publishers, 1996.

Barlow, Fred. Travail for Souls. Murfreesboro: The Sword of the Lord, October 8, 2004.

Bisagno, John. The Power of Positive Evangelism. Nashville: Broadman Press, 1968.

Blackwood, Andrew. The Preparation of Sermons. Nashville: Abingdon Press, 1968.

Breed, David R. Preparing to Preach. New York: George H. Doram Company, 1911.

Bright, Bill. The Coming Revival. Orlando: New Life Publications, 1995.

Broadus, John A. On the Preparation and Delivery of Sermons, 4th Edition. New York: Harper and Row, 1979.

Chapman, Wilbur J. The Life and Work of Dwight Lyman Moody. 1900.

Comfort, Ray. The Evidence Bible. Gainsville: Bridge-Logos Publisher, 2002.

Daniel, E.J. Dim Lights in a Dark World. Orlando: Daniels Publishing, 1971.

"Despite Urging from Leaders, SBC Falls Further Behind on Baptisms." Associated Baptist Press. 25 Apr. 2006.

Douglas, J.D., ed. The Calling of An Evangelist. Minneapolis: Worldwide Publishers, 1987.

Douglas, J.D., ed. The Work of An Evangelist. Minneapolis: Worldwide Publishers, 1984.

Drummond, Lewis. The Canvass Cathedral. Word Publishing, 2003.

Drummond, Lewis. The Evangelist. Word Publishing, 2001.

Duduit, Michael., ed. Handbook on Contemporary Preaching. Nashville: Broadman and Holman Publishers, 1992.

Duewel, Wesley. Revival Fire. Zondervan Publishing House, 1995.

Edward, Brian H. Revival. Darlington, CO: Evangelistic Press, 1990. <enduringword.com/commentaries>.

The Essential George Whitefield. www.geocities.com>.

Evans, W. Glyn. Profiles of Revival Leaders. Nashville: Broadman Press, 1976.

Finney, Charles. Lectures on Revival.

Havner, Vance. Road to Revival. New York: Fleming H. Rewell Company, MCMXL.

Hawkins, O.S. Drawing the Net. Southern Baptist Convention Annuity Board, 2002.

Hawkins, Benjamin. "Trustee Brings George Whitefield To Life for Seminary Students." <SWBTS.edu>.

Hunt, Johnny. Personal Correspondence, 19 June 2007.

Hutson, Curtis. "Prescription for Revival." Great Preaching on Revival. Vol. XVIII. Murfreesboro: Sword of the Lord Publishers, 1997.

Kentucky Baptist Convention website. 6 June 2006.

Kerr, Phil. Music in Evangelism. Glendale: Gospel Music Publishers, 1939.

Knight, Walter. Knight's Illustrations for Today. Chicago: Moody Press, 1970.

Ledbetter, Tammi Reed. "Better Equipped Than Ever but Less Effective." 29 Jan. 2007. <www.sbtexas.com>.

Leavell, Roland Q. Evangelism. Nashville: Broadman Press, 1951.

Matthews, C.E. A Church Revival. Nashville: Broadman Press, 1955.

M'Cheyne, Robert M. Sermons of Robert Murray M'Cheyne. Carlisle, Pennsylvania: The Banner of Truth Trust, 2000.

McGonigle, Huber. "Wesley Tercentenary Feature." Preacher's Magazine. Christmas 2003-2004. <nph.com>.

Morgan, G. Campbell. Evangelism. Grand Rapids: Baker Book House, 1976.

Murray, Iain. The Eighteenth Century Awakening: The Hope Revived. <Revivallibrary.org>.

Pratney, Winkie. Revival. Lafayette: Huntington House Publishing, 1984.

Rainer, Thom. Effective Evangelistic Churches. Broadman and Holman, 1998.

Rainer, Thom. "the unchurched next door." Zondervan Publishing, 2003.

Ravenhill, Leonard. Revival Praying. Minneapolis: Bethany Fellowship, 1962 <www.ravenhill.org/edwards.htm>.

Reavis, Herb, Jr. Personal Correspondence, 27 March 2007.

Reid, Alvin I. Radically Unchurched. Grand Rapids: Kregel Academics and Professional, 2003.

Rice, John. God's Work: How To Do It. Murfreesboro: Sword of the Lord Publishers, 1971.

Riley, W.B. The Soul-Winning Sermon. Murfreesboro: Sword of the Lord Publishers, 7 Nov. 2003.

Ryle, J.C. George Whitefield and His Ministry.

Scarborough, L.R. With Christ After the Lost. Nashville: Broadman Press, 1953.

Sjogren, Ping, and Pollock. Irresistable Evangelism. Loveland, California: Group Publishing, 2004.

Smith, Sheldon L., ed. Great Preaching on Revival. Murfreesboro: Sword of the Lord Publishers, 1997.

Sprague, W.B. Lectures on Revival. Ediburgh: Banner of Truth Trust, 2007.

Spurgeon, C.H. Letters To My Students. Grand Rapids: Zondervan, 1970.

Spurgeon, C.H. Spurgeon Sermons, Vol. 5. Grand Rapids: Baker House, 1999.

Spurgeon, C.H. Twelve Sermons on Decision. Grand Rapids: Baker House, 1972.

Streett, Alan. The Effective Invitation. Grand Rapids: Kregel Resources, 1984.

Stewart, James A. Heralds of God. London: Hodder and Stoughton, 1946.

Stott, John. The Cross of Christ. Leicester and Downers Grove: IVP, 1986.

Stott, John. "Fundamentalism and Evangelism." London: Crusade Booklets, 1956.

Stott, John. I Believe In Preaching. London: Hodder and Stoughton, 1982.

Stott, John. Preacher's Portrait. London: Tyrndole Press, 1961.

Sweazey, George. Effective Evangelism. New York: Harper and Row, 1953.

Towns, Elmer. Winning the Winnable. Church Leadership Institute, 1986.

Turnball, Ralph. A Treasury of D.L. Moody. Lanham, MD: University Press, 2000.

Tyson, John R. "John Wesley Remembered and More." 2003. <ChurchSociety.com>.

Walker, Alan. Standing Up To Preach. Nashville: Discipleship Resources, 1983.

Wiersbe, Warren. Bible Expository Commentary. Colorado Springs: David C. Cook Publisher, 1989.

Other Resources
by Frank Shivers

The Evangelistic Invitation 101:

150 helps in giving the evangelistic invitation

(Hard Back)
139 pages

Soul Winning 101:

275 helps for winning the lost

(Paperback)
191 pages

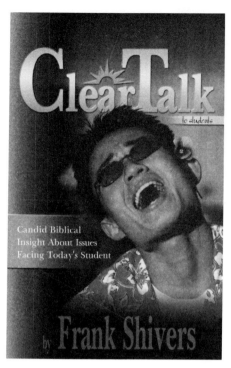

Clear Talk to Students

Candid Biblical Insight About Issues Facing Today's Student

(Paperback)
328 pages

The Pornography Trap

Clear and Candid Biblical Help Regarding Pornography for Young Men

(Booklet)
36 pages